SECRETS OF RUSTY THINGS
TRANSFORMING FOUND OBJECTS INTO ART

Michael de Meng

NORTH LIGHT BOOKS
CINCINNATI, OHIO
www.artistsnetwork.com

11 10 09 08 07   5 4 3 2 1

Distributed in Canada by Fraser Direct   .
100 Armstrong Avenue
Georgetown, ON, Canada L7G 5S4
Tel: (905) 877-4411

Distributed in the U.K. and Europe by David & Charles
Brunel House, Newton Abbot, Devon, TQ12 4PU, England
Tel: (+44) 1626 323200, Fax: (+44) 1626 323319
Email: postmaster@davidandcharles.co.uk

Distributed in Australia by Capricorn Link
P.O. Box 704, S. Windsor, NSW 2756 Australia
Tel: (02) 4577-3555

Library of Congress Cataloging-in-Publication Data

deMeng, Michael.
  Secrets of rusty things : transforming found objects into art / Michael deMeng.
      p. cm.
  Includes bibliographical references and index.
  ISBN-13: 978-1-58180-928-2 (pbk. : alk. paper)
  ISBN-10: 1-58180-928-X (pbk. : alk. paper)
  1. Handicraft. 2. Found objects (Art) I. Title.
TT149.D46 2007
745.5--dc22   2006033899

Editor: Tonia Davenport
Cover and Interior Designer: Marc Whitaker
for MTWdesign
Production Coordinator: Greg Nock
Photographers: Tim Grondin,
Christine Polomsky & OMS Photography
Cover Photo Stylist: Jan Nickum

fw
F·W PUBLICATIONS, INC.

ACKNOWLEDGMENTS

Life is like a piece of assemblage,
or a book for that matter. So many
elements from various sources contribute
to it and its integrity. I want to thank all those
who not only supplied me with rusty
things to use in my art, but more
importantly, friendship and support:
my mother and father, whose
encouragement never waivered;
Georgia Mann and Joseph Campbell,
for keeping me supplied with plenty
of comparative mythology; Don Bunse, for
convincing me to go to Mexico; and
of course, my wonderful editor,
Tonia Davenport, who not only did
a great job editing but also went to
bat for me and my ideas.

CONTENTS

NOTES FROM AN ALCHEMIST

My grandfather was an amateur magician, and periodically he would reach inside his steamer chest and retrieve something to amaze me. Salt shakers would vanish; coins would appear in my mouth; smoke would rise from his fingertips. I recall visiting magic shops with him as he enhanced his collection of secrets. When I was with him, the world was weird and wonderful and filled with everything I wanted it to be: interesting and unpredictable.

Not long after my grandfather died, I was given access to a box full of his mysteries—gizmos and instructions to create his amazing illusions. Alas, revealed secrets can have a sobering, unfulfilling quality. He used secret pockets and weighted dice to give the perception of miracles. Oh how I wished his illusions could have been truth, and perhaps I wanted this so desperately because I wished that his magic could have kept him alive a bit longer. If there was no such thing as magic, then I wished that his demise was just another bit of his hocus pocus. Of course, it wasn't hocus pocus, and suddenly my world became a little too real, a little too gray. I wanted my grandfather back. I wanted the world to be transformed from cold drab matter into radiant gold. I wanted to believe in alchemy.

Lead into gold. That is what alchemists, the early scientists, were said to have been pursuing—harnessing the divine in an attempt to do miraculous things on the earthly plane. But more than that, they too wanted the world to be a mystical place. They believed that by tapping into the unseen they could bring light and all that glistens to a dreary world.

When I envision the stereotypical alchemist, I envision a scene in which strange devices are scattered about a candlelit room. Tabletops are covered with books and bizarre scribblings; meanwhile, beakers and vials bubble and smoke with strange potions. Come to think about it, is this not my studio? Am I not an alchemist at heart? I too have similar goals of the alchemist; I am in search of clues from other less worldly places to inform my artwork. Instead of lead, I take gears, typewriters and irons, and try to transmutate these ordinary objects into something of wonder, something precious—at least to me. In my studio I can feel as if I am touching something outside myself, something inexplicable. I think this is why I have always had a fascination with mythology. Myths, like alchemy, and like art, are attempts to catch a glimpse of that undiscovered country. They take everyday existence and transform it into something remarkable. It is through these stories that misfortunes are transformed into adventures, attractions are transformed into everlasting love, and the process of life and death is transformed into a magnificent mechanism that operates beyond our line of sight.

Life can be a horribly mundane venture of paying bills, vacuuming floors, mowing lawns and cleaning toilets. For me, it is through art that I can battle the oppression of the everyday. It is in the sanctity of my studio I can become an alchemist. I can regain my sense of wonder, and here I can believe that my grandfather was capable of levitating women through the room.

One might assume, from what I have just stated, that I have definitive spiritual beliefs. Nothing could be farther from the truth. I am a seeker. I want to believe in magic realms, but I have learned that, in some ways, it doesn't really matter whether they exist or not. Illusions can be just as important as actual miracles. I doubt that any empirical data would prove that my grandfather had any special powers, but as I think back, I know he did, though it may only have been in my mind's eye. Through his illusions and tricks, he made me marvel at the world, and it is because of this I will forever be thankful. After all, he touched my heart, and what is more miraculous than that? Absolutely nothing. If I could perform the same feats of compassion through my art that he managed to accomplish through his sleight of hand, then I could claim to be an alchemist and change lead into gold.

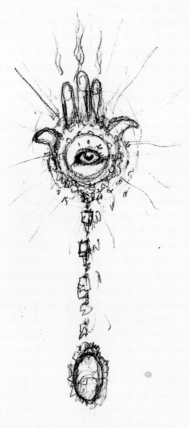

The glorious sun
Stays in his course and plays the alchemist,
Turning with splendor of his precious eye
The meager cloddy earth to glittering gold.
~WILLIAM SHAKESPEARE

HARK!

To my sister, Michelle

AMATERASU

The sun is life. All living things spinning on the third planet would have to buy into this theory. If not for its warm glow, you could forget about those summer picnics and, well, pretty much anything else. Of course, everyone knows that if the Earth circled a bit closer to this massive fiery orb, we'd be burnt toast, and were it to be a bit farther away, we'd be snow cones. This very delicate relationship between the sun and earth is a sacred one. I am unaware of any culture that views the sun in an adverse way. Usually it is the symbol of life. Sun equals good.

This is certainly true in Japan, where the sun is represented by the goddess, Amaterasu. It was said that all light emanated from her—not just physical light, but the metaphoric light associated with warmth and compassion toward all things. In contrast, she had a brother who was a bit of a jerk. Susanoo was his name and he was the god of the sea and storms. Quite a show-off, and perhaps a bit jealous of his sister's benevolent and undeniable power, he exerted his powers ever more forcefully. Now, I mentioned that Susanoo was a jerk, but I should also mention he was a bit of a snot...I mean this quite literally; he was born from his father's "nose washings." Nice.

I can't tell you how many times my sister called me a snot when we were kids (though it is quite possible she still says it, but not to my face). Isn't that the role of brothers—to be snotty to sisters? Well, Susanoo was no different, I suppose, but his aggressiveness and his jealousy of his glorious sister was pretty extreme. In some versions of this tale, Susanoo went to the underworld for a bit, and when he returned, he was somewhat jaded (as I would imagine the underworld would do to someone—that's what you get for hanging out with the wrong crowd). When he returned, the world turned to chaos from his fits of anger and aggression. To the delight of Susanoo, lightning, thunder, wind and tidal waves consumed the globe. In fact, the world became so dangerous that all living things went into hiding, though there were not many places beyond the storm god's reach.

His sister, the sun goddess, was so shocked by his transformation that she too fled into a dark cave to avoid his wrath. She moved a large boulder in front of the cave entrance for added security. Inside, the cave remained bright as daylight from her radiance, but her soul was dark and distrustful, and her hand never left her bow and quiver in the event her brother attempted to seek her out.

Suddenly, the world was without Amaterasu's benevolent light, and the universe grew very dim. This concerned the other gods, who feared that not only the earth but the entire universe would fall into stormy chaos. They pleaded with the sun goddess to return to her rightful place in the sky, but Amaterasu's fear of her brother was too severe.

Meanwhile, the goddess of the dawn and revelry, Ama-no-Uzume, was a little sick and tired of all this doom and gloom (as would be the case with a party goddess). Enough was enough. A goddess of action, Ama-no-Uzume took a mirror and hung it on a tree that faced the entrance to the cave. Then she stripped herself of all of her clothes, took a tub, turned it over and started to dance on it. She was having a grand time despite the dark skies overhead. The other gods saw this strange spectacle and broke out in hysterics and delight. They created such a joyful commotion that when Amaterasu heard the laughing she was shocked and bewildered. "What could be so funny in a dark world?" she wondered. So she pushed the boulder away from the entrance to have a "look-see," and as she did, she caught a glimpse of herself in the mirror. She was struck with a beam of her intense, beautiful light and was so startled that the other gods managed to block her as she attempted to retreat into the cave. However, Amaterasu was still fearful of her crazed brother. Collectively, the gods agreed that Susanoo would be punished, and upon hearing this, the sun goddess returned to the heavens, blessing the world with her glow of life and light.

As for her brother, he was kicked out of heaven for his antics; after all, boogers can't be choosers.

Okay, I have just spent an hour attempting to find the original source of the "light-bulb-over-someone's-head" image, thinking that it might be a nice segue as I delve into the post-myth discussion. While I didn't uncover too much information, one thing is obvious—it wasn't around before Edison. Pre-Edison, this concept was not a light bulb, but a ray of light; it was a halo, or an aura. The reason this image is so important is that it is the symbol of a bright idea—an inspired idea. Rays of sunlight emanated from the individual because he had been touched by something divine. Ultimately, I see it as the same premise.

The myth of Amaterasu is a myth that really speaks of the importance of illumination (a.k.a., inspiration), an idea much discussed by artists. It is a mystical force that comes from some unknown place. I can't tell you the number of times I have been at work in the studio, attempting to resolve some work of art, yet trapped in frustration and darkness. I have to admit this happens more often than I would like, but most of the time, right before I smash the piece to smithereens, something otherworldly pops into my head, a bit of magic intervenes to offer guidance to the dilemma. I should note that sometimes, smashing the piece to smithereens is the necessary guidance—the destruction that opened the door for illumination.

Finding inspiration amidst frustration and darkness is not unlike the story of the sun goddess. The world is in despair (a metaphor for a struggling artist attempting to find resolution). The darkness of uncertainty weighs heavier and heavier. Things grow stormier and stormier. Nothing is working. It is at this point that Amaterasu steps in, but not without some coaxing. I believe that such divine intervention occurs when one has nothing left to lose. One suddenly has *carte blanche* to break rules or attempt the unheard of. This is what coaxed Amaterasu out of her cave: desperation, absurdity and, sure enough, the result was the light of knowledge—the boulder is moved from the cave.

Amaterasu is an entity that resides in all of us. As an artist, it is in the studio that I seek her guidance the most. I work until that light bulb goes on. I don't mind that deities have converted to incandescent bulbs in place of sunlight. I'm just glad that idea bulbs don't come in those lousy fluorescent tubes. (Too noisy.)

LETTING DAYLIGHT OUT

I don't always start with a sketch, but in this case it seems important. I'm starting with a weird, 1970s clock-shape as the base, but it's very powerful, and I need to do a little figuring as to how to tone it down. The last thing in the world

I want is a piece that looks like it would be hanging in the Brady living room . . . or even worse, Greg Brady's groovy attic pad. (Remember that episode with the love beads?) I'm going to have to do something to draw less attention to the spires. They need to be sun-like, but they need

CLOCK—The term "estate sale" cracks me up. Whenever I go garage-saling, I'll hear the term used and get very excited. In my mind, I imagine a grand old manor, like Wayne Manor

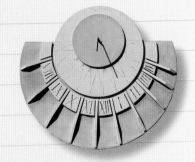

to feel like the rays emanating from something powerful . . . like Amaterasu.

in "Batman." I envision piles of antiques and ornate fixtures that are selling for pennies on the dollar.

The reality is a bit different. Estate sales are typically filled with bad motel paintings of seashores, strange 1970s candleholders, piles of cassette (or 8-track) tapes and an inexplicable amount of spatulas. The funny thing is that I know what I am typically in for, but I still can't shake my disappointment when I pull up the driveway and see the oversized wooden spoons and

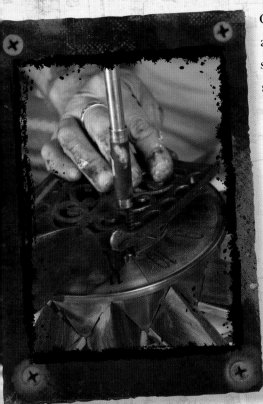

Okay, the sketches are only getting me so far. They don't seem to be helping. Sometimes you have to just hunker down and start assembling. Truth is, I can only do so much planning. I have to get my hands dirty. I have to get them rusty. Looking. Looking. When in doubt,

11

always use an iron form. They are great because they have a shrine shape built into them. Of course, this is an iron thing that is not an actual iron but some vintage thing that holds an iron (maybe). Well, it's cool, whatever it is, and it belongs in the center of the groovy clock. This will be the cave of the sun goddess—the place she'll hide from her nasty bro.

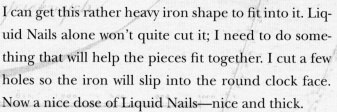

Time for Dremel action. I can find any reason to use the cut-off blade. (I like the sparks.) In this case, I need to cut a hole in the clock so I can get this rather heavy iron shape to fit into it. Liquid Nails alone won't quite cut it; I need to do something that will help the pieces fit together. I cut a few holes so the iron will slip into the round clock face. Now a nice dose of Liquid Nails—nice and thick.

As usual, my hands are covered with the stuff. So I wipe them off on my pants. My painting pants are a sight to behold. They started off as cargo paints, but through months and months of Liquid Nails and paint, they are more like leather chaps. A nice coating of adhesives has made them fairly solid. I look

at it as protection for my quadriceps. A stray Dremel or power drill would have a tough time cutting through this fabric. Hmmm . . . perhaps I'll market this idea.

So . . . now what? An iron on a Brady clock. It's still too groovy. Not to mention, a tough shape. I have always felt that the circle is a difficult form to tackle because the shape can be so strong that the art can become secondary. I wonder if that is the reason

This certifies that the fire equipment was serviceable condition on the date noted.

forks proudly displayed on the tables in the garage. So, one has to be a bit creative when it comes to these type of sales. You can usually find some killer deals, but typically it's deals on things no one would want anyway.

I remember being at one such estate sale, the "Brady Bunch" house through and through. I'm sure it was very stylish at the time, but time apparently stopped, and never moved again. The walls were olive green with orange trim. The kitchen had some nicely painted poop-brown cupboards. I think they figured that if they waited long enough, the style would come back in fashion. It probably would.

I couldn't find anything. I wandered and wandered, but nothing seemed to catch my eye. Then I saw it: a clock. The most 1970s clock one could imagine. In fact, I think my parents may have had one themselves. It was

13

religious mandalas are so intricate. Perhaps all the designs force the attention away from the circle-ness.

The iron "cave" needs something beneath it; something that will draw more attention to it rather than to those blasted rays of sunshine. Man, they are tough to tone down. An oven thermometer? No, too subtle. Looking around . . . there's the ticket! Something that I have had around for years; a strange light fixture, complete with leafy forms and a nice tube protrusion that will visually break through the lower portion of the circle. In fact, it was obviously used in some other

piece of artwork before, because my painting designs are all over it. Strange thing is, I have no idea what it was part of. Something recent? For the life of me, I can't recall. Doesn't matter; it has a new job now.

I swear those spires are going to be the death of me. It's very bizarre to me that as I work on a piece of art, I form a relationship with it. The relationship evolves through the process. Usually it starts off innocently enough, then, either the piece is pleasant and amiable or it is contentious and uncooperative. In fact, I seem to have inner dialogues with the piece as I work.

one of those clocks that had sun-like metal spires shooting out of it. The only thing it needed was a couple of those oversized, lava rock cigarette lighters to go beneath it. Of course, I had no idea what on earth I would do with it. I never do. One thing was for sure: there was absolutely no way anyone else was going to buy the thing, so I saved it from a slow death at the landfill.

SECONDHAND STORE

IRON THINGY — A Missoula secondhand store—which I wont identify by name. They had

plenty of interesting items for sale, but it was somewhat intimidating when you walked in. I was greeted (greeted is generous— whats the opposite of greeted?) by one of the owners, a sixty-some-year-old woman sitting behind a counter listening to a police

The dialogue for this piece is going something like this: "What if I do this to you?" It replies, "Sure you can do that . . . if you want me to look like crap."

I turn to some painting. The painting can help bring it all together; a bit of color might give me the direction I need. So I go for a yellow. It *is* a myth about the sun. Well, I have to say there is a reason that I don't use pure yellow all that much. Not really my cup of tea. Let's ignore the yellow for now and add a few deMengian squiggles and dots. Very nice . . . NOT!

Sometimes my relationship with my artwork during the creative process is like two lovers, where everything is magical and falls right into place. More often, however, it is like two very opinionated personalities trying to assert dominance. The sun goddess is being very stubborn, and I wonder what in the world she wants from me. I know that she wants to be a really cool piece, but she's not helping me find the solution.

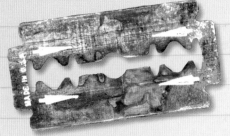

Unfortunately, this process is reminding me of the myth the work is supposed to represent. The question is, how will I coax the sun goddess to come forth? I need to do a little dance on a washtub. Actually, what I really need is a drink, but it's only ten in the morning. I believe a quadruple macchiato will have to do the trick.

Ah. Nice to be away. I learned a long time ago that if you don't get away from the artwork when things start to go wrong, you will spend hours and hours being frustrated and potentially screwing everything up more and more and more. I end up not coming back for the rest of the day.

scanner. She would look you up and down as you walked in the door, sizing you up and figuring out if you were the shoplifting sort. She had signs all over the joint: "don't touch," "you break it, you buy it," etc.

I was looking for frames—nothing fancy, just gaudy, old picture frames. I was hesitant to go in. I hated it in there, but none of the other secondhand stores had what I was looking for. So I walked past her police scanner gauntlet. I was in!

I looked around and came across an interesting item; for lack of a better word it was a strange iron thingy. It was old and apparently fit over an iron; beyond that, I have no idea what it was for. Perhaps it was something to set the iron on? In any event, it was very interesting-looking, and I liked it, so I set it up at the counter.

17

The next morning, I take a half-hour shower. The reason for the long shower is that I do most of my best thinking in there. I can usually resolve most of my artistic dilemmas under a stream of hot water. With the water beating on my head, I envision the work. There she is, the sun goddess and her cursed spires. Now I'm having a conversation with my shower god. "Make the spires less important," it says. "How?" I ask. "Duh. Run an object through them that will break up the linear quality of each spike. Maybe wire, maybe rope. Hey, don't you have that round piece of metal in your studio? You know, the one you got from the scrap yard." The light bulb goes on.

I pile through my bins. Where is that thing? I just saw it. It's just where I left it: on the very bottom of that box filled with heavy, oily, metal gears. I decide to tie the metal circle to the spires with twine. The twine will add another element that will draw attention away from the rays. Twelve wrappings later, it is attached. Perfect. It totally did what the shower god said it would do. Thank you, shower god.

I need to figure out what I want to do for the Amaterasu image. I need a woman's face, so it is time for the encyclopedia/magazine/book leafing process. It is not unheard of for me to spend

Back to look for the frames. There was an enormous bin of paintings with horrible (and I mean horrible) art. Most of the paintings had come out of the frames, which didn't bother me. I just wanted the frames—she could

have the paintings. I grabbed about ten frames and brought them to the counter.

The owner said, "Those have paintings that go with them." "Yes, I know, but I only want the frames. I'll pay the same price, and you can still have the paintings to sell." (Yeah right— like someone would really buy

hours looking for the right image. It seems like such a simple process, but as I mentioned, sometimes artwork can be very opinionated and doesn't want just any old image adorning it. The sun goddess has been difficult so far, so I figure this process will be no different.

What do you know? The first image I find seems to jive. Maybe my relationship with the work has changed. Maybe the sun goddess wants to cooperate. Time to come back to the yellow. That will tell all. I need to tone it down. After all, I don't want this to be a big smiley-face sun. That's not really my style.

Let's try a light wash of Dioxazine Purple. Most people don't know that using a complementary color as a wash can really do wonders. In this case, I wouldn't say wonders,

those things.) Regardless, what would she care? She would still be getting the same amount. Wrong. She did care. "Oh, no," she said, "I have to go through that bin and match the paintings with the frames. I'm not going to sell those without the paintings." I reiterated that I would pay the same amount with or without the painting. Nope.

I was dumbfounded. I put all the frames back in the bin and debated whether or not I would purchase the iron thingy. Out of pride, I wasn't going to, but I decided it was too cool to pass up. So I bought it, and I'll never return again.

but it does tone it down a bit. What I need is a different color. Something shockingly different on top of the yellow. What to use? What to use? I just have to be gutsy and add something. Maybe some coppery green will help. Finally, she is starting to come out from her cave.

A few more washes, some more little details and there she is. The sun goddess has finally come out. Not bad. Might have to add a thing or two, but at least she's in view. Took her long enough. Now it's time for that drink. Make it a double.

To Cindy

DONAJI

In the 1970s Patrick Flanagan coined the phrase "pyramid power." His theory was that the pyramids of ancient Egypt had supernatural powers. Although the Egyptians are often considered *the* builders of pyramids, high above the Oaxaca countryside in southern Mexico sits the ancient city and pyramids of the Zapotec people. I'm not sure if these pyramids offered the same mystical powers that Patrick Flanagan promoted, but they did offer the advantage of being able to see one's adversaries from miles away. The pyramid-topped fortress of Monte Albán was a two-thousand-year project. (The next time your remodel runs behind schedule, remember: It could be worse.)

The bummer for the Zapotecs was that after two thousand years of toiling and designing what turned out to be a pretty cool place, a rival people, the Mixtecs, managed to take control of Monte Albán, thus giving them the "pyramid power," and that is where our story begins . . .

In the town of Zaachila, a Zapotec child was born. No ordinary child, this was Princess Donaji, daughter to King Cosijoeza. It was a joyous day for the king, but not for long. Soon after Donaji's birth, the king received a visit from a revered and insightful Zapotec priest. He had come from the city of Mitla, "place of the dead," to inform the king of a bittersweet omen regarding the princess. According to the stars, Donaji would sacrifice her life for her people. Not exactly the type of news a father wants to hear on what is supposed to be a joyous day of passing out cigars, or whatever it was they passed out back then.

Years passed, Donaji grew into a beautiful woman and the battles between the Zapotecs and the Mixtecs continued. King Cosijoeza had hoped to regain Monte Albán for his people, but attempt after attempt failed. After one particularly violent Zapotec defeat, King Cosijoeza, with his daughter, Donaji, approached the Mixtec prince, Nucano, to surrender.

Nucano was young and handsome, and Donaji fell in love with him upon first sight. A mutual experience occurred with Nucano, one of those Dean Martin, when-the-moon-hits-your-eye-like-a-big-pizza-pie moments. So smitten was Nucano, he decided to offer peace with the Zapotecs, on the condition that Donaji be held hostage at Monte Albán,

as insurance for the treaty. Donaji immediately agreed, but King Cosijoeza resisted. Nucano assured the Zapotec lord that Donaji would be treated as a queen and would be granted every luxury possible, including her safety.

Cosijoeza realized that this was the moment of his daughter's foretold sacrifice, but that perhaps the sacrifice didn't mean her death; rather, it was a sacrifice resulting in her leaving her people. He would miss his daughter, but . . . this grand gesture would save many lives, so Cosijoeza agreed to the terms.

Years of peace passed by, and Nucano was true to his word, offering the princess benefits befitting a queen. Donaji was quite happy, but her heart never fully left her people, and more and more she found herself homesick for what she had left behind. Adding to her wounds was the fact that she lived atop Monte Albán, the ancient capital of her people. Every building was a reminder of the mastery of art, science and engineering the Zapotecs had achieved—centuries of labor swiped in mere moments. This made her bitter, even toward Nucano.

One evening, the prince departed Monte Albán in the cloak of night. Donaji pondered. With Nucano away, this was a moment of opportunity for the Zapotecs. She was torn. Her love had not diminished for Nucano, but was her love stronger for her people? Yes. On that night, she bribed a servant to deliver a message to her father of the Mixtecs' vulnerability.

Cosijoeza ordered his armies to attack the Mixtecs. Unfortunately, the Zapotecs were defeated, even with the warrior prince away. Of course, on returning home, Nucano was furious. And it didn't take long for Nucano to figure out what happened. The prince wept, for he knew what needed to be done.

The Zapotecs heard rumors of Donaji's execution, but they never found her body. Several months later, a Zapotec shepherd was wandering by the river when he came across a beautiful purple iris growing on the bank. He went to examine it and found that the flower was growing in the ear of a severed head. It was Princess Donaji, who still seemed alive. The magic of pyramid power.

So, you may be wondering right now why it is I even bothered to mention pyramids at the beginning of the Donaji story. Well, I think pyramids are an important aspect of the tale, and not just because they remain in the Zapotec ruins. Pyramids are a tremendous metaphor; they are a metaphor for the search for truth. Ever look at the back of a dollar bill and see the big ol' eye sitting on top of the pyramid? Well, that is supposed to represent (according to the Masons) the eye of God, the eye that is able to see in all directions at all times. If one is below the pyramid, one can see only a certain perspective, but on top lies truth and clarity.

Okay, so what has this to do with art and Donaji? Well, Donaji is a symbol of sacrifice to find truth. In many ways, she is like Prometheus, stealing fire from the gods but suffering the consequences for the betterment of humanity. In her case, it was for the betterment of her people. She wanted to bring them metaphoric truth.

I believe, and I suppose you could call me a bit biased on this topic, that Donaji is the story of what I like to consider the ideal artist, an artist whose main motivation is the search for truth. Of course, I can see how a cynic might question the artist's role as a self-sacrificing seeker of truth. After all, is that what artists do? Well, I contend that beauty without truth is hollow and trite, and it seems to me that the concept of pure truth could be nothing but beautiful.

You see, artists are in a special position, because they are often willing to see and then express things that others dare not. They're always looking forward, or more appropriately, they are always climbing up and then returning to share what they have seen.

So it is true with Donaji. She climbed, she saw and she sacrificed. Don't get me wrong, I would certainly be content keeping my head on my shoulders, but any artist willing to explore new ideas is placing her head on a metaphoric chopping block. The question is whether the viewer will notice the flower of insight growing from your ear before or after the hatchet falls.

BELOW THE PYRAMIDS

Most of my junk is kept safe and dry, but there some objects that I keep outside in the Land of Forgotten Junk. I don't venture out there often, but sometimes I get desperate. Today is one such day.

Outside, amidst the old VCR and golf clubs, I find the metal insert to a toolbox. I didn't really think that it could be used for anything, though I have proven that line of thinking to be wrong time and time again. A couple of cuts with the Dremel on one of the short sides, a bend or two, and I could have myself a perfect shrine shape.

PORT TOWNSEND WORKSHOP

IRON—*There are certain advantages to being an assemblage instructor. Yes, it's true I can steal all the great ideas that my students have and use them in my work. But, the really great thing about being an instructor of the assemblage realm is that instead of apples, students will often bring me found objects to use in my work. Recently, a student gave me a jar full of cocoons (empty, of course). In another class I received a handful of optometrist lenses, and another student mailed me twenty pounds of oily metal gears. Way better than some wormy apple.*

While I'm rummaging, I also find the remnants of a grandfather clock that I once had big plans for. Now it has more or less disintegrated through three or so Montana winters. All that is left are some pieces of wood that might work out. Or, might not.

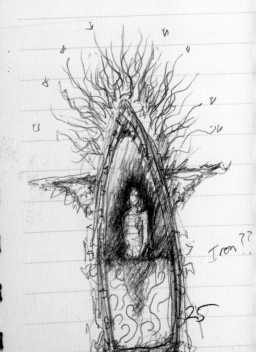

Iron ??

25

I start laying the parts out. I have some decorative dowels that someone left behind after a class I taught. The only thing I know for sure is that I'm going to use that great decayed iron that was given to me. It has a nice mountain/pyramid/shrine quality that goes with the story. I screw, glue and nail everything into place, and then blast some foam insulation around the objects, and I start to sing "Oh, it's drying time again . . . " In the interim, I decide it's an opportune time to head to Home Resource.

Home Resource is a salvage artist's dream. It's a recycling center where people can donate their junk from a remodel or demolition. Everything and anything that you could imagine being in a house (sans furnishings, that is) is available. Normally, this stuff would end up in the landfill, but these guys recycle it for amazingly low prices. I usually walk around and fill up a box with random items, and at most it might cost me five to ten dollars. Of course, I think they give me the assemblage-artist discount. They have a great annual event called SpoCon (Spontaneous Construction) in which artists are

given from noon to 5 p.m. to create a found-object masterpiece. They bill it as *Junkyard Wars* meets *Extreme Home Makeover*. They're a pretty cool clan, never forgeting the arts . . . of course, Missoula is that kind of town in general. I purchase my five dollar box o' junk and head back to the studio.

A day later, everything is nice and dry. A bit of foam whittling and then a few washes of paint for inspiration. I find a nice coppery green that works well.

I love my Dremel tool, and yes, maybe I love it so much that I will marry it. Funny thing is that it's only within the last couple of years that I actu-

Last year, I was teaching in Port Townsend and a student (who we will call "Stacie" because that is her name) arrived at class early with a surprise for me. Stacie had been in a few classes of mine prior to this venue, so she knew my work and the types of discarded goodies that twist my knobs. She handed me something that was, I must admit, one of the coolest things I had ever seen. It was an old interior of an iron, which doesn't sound that interesting, but what was amazing was how it had decomposed. The metal had deteriorated in such a way that made it look more like rock than metal. It was beautiful. I thanked Stacie profusely and stashed it away.

One thing about my classes is that the first few minutes are a scavenging free-for-all. I bring boxes of junk for people to rummage through, and this class was no different; students battled each other for the best junk while I turned up the volume of "Anarchy in the U.K.," by the Sex Pistols, to set the mood.

ally have owned one. I fell in love with the device when a student of mine brought one to class. I immediately rushed out to purchase one. It has never left my side since.

Bear in mind, I am not the savviest cat when it comes to using all of the various Dremel attachments. I leave the grinding, etching and buffing to others. For me, it is all about cutting through all types of things, especially metal.

I have to slice through some metal bands. In the old days, I would mess around with metal snips or blast through blade after blade with a jigsaw. Now, the Dremel is easy and comes with its own taste of adventure—sparks! Who needs fireworks when there is metal to be cut? As for the danger, well, let's just say I won't be putting any unprotected eyes in front of those pretty sparks. For the record, pretty sparks are hot, flying metal shards. Unless you're going for the pirate look, goggles are crucial.

It's time for some decorative painting—my trademark spermy shapes and watery patterns. The reason I incorporate some of this type of imagery in every single piece of my work is because it is a nice way to soften the tactile. Painted designs always strike me as mystical. This might be because repetitive designs are so prevalent in sacred art forms. I find using these designs brings a different dimension to the various

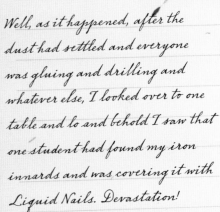

found objects. The everyday items begin to transcend into a different realm. I find that painted designs help take an object like an iron and make the "iron" as we know it less apparent. Instead, the shape is the most relevant component in such a work of art.

Well, as it happened, after the dust had settled and everyone was gluing and drilling and whatever else, I looked over to one table and lo and behold I saw that one student had found my iron innards and was covering it with Liquid Nails. Devastation!

I was faced with an immediate quandary. I could either take the piece back and say that it wasn't meant for class consumption, or I could let it slide, as disappointing as that might have been. It seemed quite unteacherly to yank an object from someone when I just got through a speech about hunting and gathering for cool junk. I decided to take the attitude that it was all part of the found object game. Someone's loss is someone else's gain, finders keepers, and all of that tripe.

29

This

I add more doodads. A plastic heart, some wires that grow like vines out of the iron—perhaps like lilies? In fact, I think I'll paint some vine-like shapes on a scale form to really help bring the myth into play.

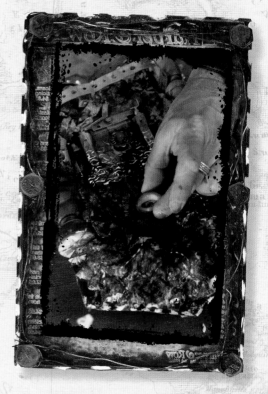

The iron shape is supposed to represent the mountain fortress of Monte Albán—in particular, the pyramids. Having worked for tips a good number of years as a bartender and having seen my share of dollar bills, I can't envision a pyramid without an eye above it. I think an "Eye of God" on the iron would be kind of an interesting play of ideas. I find a really nice round lens (almost an entire half sphere), and then attach an eye image behind it. It is placed on the shrine/iron/pyramid.

Here's the skinny with my eye fetish. It took me a number of years to figure out, and I can't believe I never realized it sooner, but when I was a kid, my grandfather had a contact lens business, Crown Contact Lens. Whenever I visited my grandparents, I would always get to have colored eyes. Sometimes purple, sometimes aqua, sometimes one brown and one green. Everywhere in the office were eye charts and anatomical images. Even their logo was a big eye.

As it turned out, the student struggled (I mean really struggled). She was having a hell of a time, and in particular, she was having a hell of a time because the iron was too heavy for what she wanted to do. It was a structural engineering problem for someone not ready for such a complicated undertaking. At this point, the dark side of déMeng saw a prime opportunity to retrieve what was rightfully his. I had to act quickly . . .

Oh, the mental angst! Well, I was faced with two options: help her make the iron work (which would have been no small task), or recommend that she abandon the iron for something more manageable. The choice was clear. I turned into Darth déMeng—I really wanted the iron back, even though it was covered in gook; after all, I knew a few minutes under a propane torch would restore it rightfully to its original decayed grandeur.

If I helped her, I betrayed the artist in me. One the other hand,

Earlier in the day, I came across an image in an encyclopedia of an Armenian girl. I know, I know, Donaji was Zapotec, but the reason I was struck with it was that the girl looked just like she could have lived in the Oaxaca valley. Taking the photo, I burn the edges with a match, and then I place the burnt image onto the iron. I bring some water patterns through her face to give the effect that her head is partially underwater, then I extend the water patterns past the paper and into the surrounding objects. By moving a pattern through various forms, you can help unify things that normally wouldn't go together. The piece is really looking done to me, but I'd like to give it some time to sink in . . . no pun intended.

It's morning, and I have my cup of joe in hand. Let's have a fresh look . . . Is it finished? Nope, not done. Do I know why? Nope.

Next morning. I have a brainstorm. The problem is that it is too boxy. This is a romantic, spiritual tale, and it should reach beyond the boundaries of the work itself. It needs to fly out of the box frame. I happen to have a piece of wood that came from the clock. It would

by selfishly encouraging her
to discard the iron, I betrayed
the teacher in me, as well as my
philosophy of never becoming
covetous of "things." But I really,
really wanted it!

So I decide to give her the option.
It was out of my hands. It was in
the hands of the universe and fate.
If I was meant to have it, then I
would have it. I told her all of

actually be ideal for wing forms. Maybe some paint on the wings. Now I think I have the ticket. If the finished article doesn't gradually start to annoy me over the next month or so, I'll know I have a winner.

the structural steps necessary to
make the piece function the way
she envisioned. Suddenly, the
clouds parted. "That's too much
work," she said. Hallelujah!
My ethics remained intact . . .
somewhat. Oh well, losers weepers.

To George

34

FACE OF GLORY

Shiva is an interesting deity. Like most Hindu gods, he comes complete with multiple arms and beautiful blue skin. His moniker is "Shiva the Destroyer," and he's responsible for shaking up the universe when it needs a change; thus destruction is not necessarily a bad thing.

There is an interesting story involving Shiva and his wife, Parvati. (No, not the story where Shiva beheads Parvati's son, Ganesha, and then restores him with the head of an elephant. Perhaps in another book, we can get into that one.) This story involves a greedy king, Jalandhara.

Jalandhara was a giant who had conquered most of the world, and he decided that he fancied Parvati. Now, it's a little unclear if the king was motivated by lust, power or hubris. I suppose a conquering giant was just used to getting what it wanted. Devising a plot, Jalandhara decided he would abduct Shiva's bride. Now, Shiva was no little dude—he was a major deity. Granted, the king was a giant, but that was nothing compared to the power of the Destroyer, so Jalandhara decided he might need a little assistance.

I imagine the next scene fresh out of a Humphrey Bogart film, in a dark, smoky bar. The king interviewed a variety of shady characters to be his heavy. Ogres of all shapes and sizes came to apply for the job, all with quite extensive (and oftentimes quite brutal) resumes. A tough decision, until Jalandhara was approached by a rather large, mean-looking monster named Rahu.

What was most impressive about this demon was his audacity. The king was quite familiar with Rahu's endeavor to swallow the moon. Over and over, Rahu had attempted to swallow this rather large celestial object, and he would have succeeded, except for one thing: Rahu had no stomach. Needless to say, because of this strange biological trait, the moon always escaped, resulting merely in a lunar eclipse.

Jalandhara considered this applicant for a moment. The monster seemed mean enough and determined enough, and the lack of stomach might have been beneficial in that if Rahu, in his rage, accidentally devoured the abducted Parvati, she wouldn't be permanently consumed. Perfect. Rahu was hired.

There are reasons why major deities were major deities. They tended to pay attention to what was happening around them. Sometimes it was because they had spies and servants looking out for their best interest, and sometimes it was because they had great intuitive powers, but usually it was a bit of both. When Shiva learned of the evil plot, he became so enraged that the mere furling of the great god's brow created a creature with fiery eyes, a lion's mouth and a never-ending hunger. Shiva ordered this creation to devour Rahu, who attempted to flee this incarnation of Shiva's wrath. Of course, Rahu was no match for the creature, and moments before Rahu was about to be devoured, he turned to Shiva and begged for mercy.

It should be known that in the Hindu belief system, if anyone pleads for mercy, a deity cannot deny it. So Shiva ordered the ravenous monster to cease the attack. Extremely relieved, Rahu thanked the great deity. Shiva's manifestation was a little less than pleased, however, and protested, "Shiva, you created me, and more than that, you made me hungry. What do you expect me to eat now?"

Shiva looked around. The creation had a point. It was pretty big, and to allow it to be hungry was risky. Who knows what it might eat. Unlike Rahu, this thing had a stomach, so if it decided to eat the moon, for instance, the moon wouldn't come back. Shiva pondered for a moment and said, "Eat your hands and your feet."

This seemed reasonable to the creature, and so he began to devour his feet and his hands. He was so hungry, though, that he didn't stop there. He continued to eat his entire body until all that was left was his face.

Shiva watched this in amazement and declared, "This is my most magnificent creation! From this day forward, it shall be known as Kirttimukha, the Face of Glory, and must always remain at the entrance of my door. From now on, nobody comes before me, before first bowing to Kirttimukha."

Who is this strange demon Kirttimukha? Mere desire or an insatiable appetite? And why was Shiva so smitten with him? This is not a cautionary tale of the consequences of gluttony. I don't see this as a tale of a self-consuming Pac-Man. (I must confess, however, that a Kirttimukha/Pac-Man video game is kind of a cool idea.) I think that what Shiva saw in the ravenous Kirttimukha was one of the universe's most profound ironies: life must devour itself to survive—a recognition that for growth, there must be destruction. The tale of Kirttimukha is similar to the story of Oroburos, an ancient snake who swallowed his own tail and formed a circle in the process. The world is in a perpetual state of creation and annihilation, neither of which could occur without the other. To live one must die, yin and yang, lightness and dark. You get the picture. Shiva loved a dark comedy, and this is one of the greatest.

I often think of Shiva as I dismantle a typewriter, or VCR, or clock . . . There is a line in the Hindu scripture Bhagavad Gita that states something to the effect of, "I am to become death, the shatterer of worlds." With my sledgehammer in hand, I become the hand of time. Not a dealer in death in a literal sense, but I become the destroyer of previous universes and previous existences. With each turn of the screwdriver, each drop of the hammer, the functions of the past are disassembled to ruin. (As a side note, I must say that when taking apart a typewriter, the only way to describe the process is ruin—including what's left of your bloody knuckles.) What starts as a Zen process of removing bolts and screws eventually evolves into frustration and, ultimately, the sound of smashing metal.

From the bolts and gears and strange thingamajigs, new lives are born. More often than not, the various parts are scattered hither and yon, reborn as art. At some point, these art forms, scattered hither and yon, will too be dismantled—whether by design or the hand of time—and once again will arise to a new existence.

This is what is implicit in the tale of Kirttimukha. The mouth of the universe nourishes and creates itself, but at its own expense. When I work, I devour and annihilate the past, and by doing so, I create room for the future. I am Kirttimukha. It is the story of all artists. It is the story of all living things.

As Pablo Picasso said, "Every act of creation is first an act of destruction."

SELF-CONSUMED

There are some great versions of Kirttimukha carved into the sides of Hindu temples. Most of them consist of a very wide-faced monster; the monster is actually somewhat comical and could even be mistaken for a Muppet (the one that comes to mind is Animal, the drummer). The Kirttimukhas I am most smitten with are missing a lower jaw, or at least it isn't visible; this is because the Face

of Glory is filling its face with itself. Many of these carvings have a circular design. In the center is the face of Kirttimukha. Around the big monster, designs seem to flow down around his large face and then disappear up into his mouth. All of life goes there. This is the effect that I want.

I need a circular form, so I pick an oval frame I have lying about. Next I need a monster's face. After a long debate with myself, I opt to begin with a human mask form. For this, I consider a variety of options, including a more monstrous, bestial

DEPARTMENT STORE

HANDS — Mannequin parts are sometimes easy to come by. Other times, they require cold, hard cash. Typically, I don't like to reach into my wallet if I know I can acquire something for free. Okay, so it pays to know someone in the retail clothing biz. Usually someone in charge of displays can hook me up nicely with busted-up parts that have seen better days. In fact, I have a creepy child mannequin that has been lurking around my studio for years from such a source. I have yet to incorporate this armless entity into a work of art, but it has been painted red for a Halloween party gone by, and now it is complete with horns and a severe widow's peak. I call him Damien. One can often find limbs lying about on the Internet, but usually they come with a cost, not the least of which is shipping.

The pair of hands comes from way back. They are hands that have been stashed away, waiting for the right incarnation. The original

37

mask (Halloween's just around the corner), and a mask of that sort would be easy to come by. I toss this idea right away, because it seems that if I were to add various objects to the mask, it would become monstrous anyway, so why bother buying a specialized mask just to hid it? The mask I decide on is one of those white unadorned ones, available in craft stores. It does need to have the lower jaw removed, so a quick slice with the craft knife does the trick.

A pair of mannequin hands have been peeking out of a large box for years and have yet to be used. Not a day goes by when I don't notice those long, pointy fingers reaching out of the box. I think I might have a use for them today. Kirttimukha will devour the hands. Here's where it gets tricky. How to do this without making it look too serial-killer-esque? I know the idea of consuming one's self is a creepy premise to begin with, but actually having the hands visibly swallowed might be a bit overboard. I am tempted to ditch the hands altogether, but I decide that without them, the whole concept of life being cannibalistic is lost. And besides, if not hands, what would I use? Feet? Ears? Spleens? Hands definitely seem like the best answer to this dilemma.

acquisition of these appendages occurred over fifteen years ago . . . can that be right? I guess so. I was in my final year of art school and was working on large, mixed-media canvases. What I really needed was a bunch of jumbled body parts for the piece. What is a college student to do? Hit the pavement, and hit the big clothing stores.

As it worked out, I went into The Bon Marché and noticed a cute girl working at the counter. Well, she seemed like she might be helpful. So I approached her and said, "I have kind of a strange thing to ask." She paused, not quite sure where I was going with this. I continued, "I'm looking for mannequin parts." She sort of smiled and said in a nervous sort of way, "Why do you need those?" It was at this point that I started wondering what she must think of me, asking such a question. Did she think

The hands are laid out in relation to the face in a variety of different poses. I decide I can use them if—and only if—I can find just the right gesture. At first, I have the fingers pointing down. Nope, too much like some ghoul in a Boris Karloff movie. Then, I try the fingers in the mouth; looks like a nail-biting ogre. How about just the fingertips peeking out of the mouth? They look like weird tusks. Ultimately, I find the only solution is to have the wrists coming out of the mouth and the fingers to form a flower-like shape around the face. The hands become lotus petals. As monstrous as the scene might be, the gesture seems to soften the blow somewhat.

One thing that is going to be essential is that the Face of Glory really needs to seem like it, and all the objects around it must be one in the same. After all, he represents the totality of life—the life cycle. I use some foam insulation around the face to help it relate to the oval frame. After the foam dries, I texturize it by tearing and cutting into it.

Not just any old eyes will do for this creature. First off, if I use something too serious, it falls into the creepy zone. If I use eyes that are too be-

nevolent it still falls into the creepy zone, because then it becomes clown creepy. The only solution is to make the face a bit more surreal, a bit more toy-like with found objects. I try out a pair of opera glasses to put in place of the eyes. I do this, and I must admit that even with the opera glasses, it is a bit scary. Now I'm not sure I know what to do. Well, I'm going for it anyway. The glasses are it. If they don't work, I'll rip them off later and try something else. Really, it comes down to me coming to grips with the fact that this myth ain't pretty, albeit interesting. Such is life.

I was some depraved sex-fiend-serial-killer type? I immediately clarified and explained I was an art student working on a project... blah blah blah (which, by the way, is probably the same line that depraved sex-fiend-serial-killer types use). Well, she bought my story and said to check back after she talked to her boss.

A day or so went by, and I went back to the stores. Sure enough, Suzanne (the girl) was working. She saw me walk in and gave me the "just a second" gesture. She ran in the back and returned with a large box filled with arms, hands and feet. I was in heaven. I thanked her kindly and headed down the road.

Now to answer the obvious question: Did I get her phone number? Indeed I did.

LISBON FLEA MARKET

OPERA GLASSES – *Sometimes you have to pay the piper, and*

Chains are attached to the mouth and dangle down. I do this because one of the Kirttimukha carvings that stuck in my head seemed to have a river flowing into or out of his mouth. The chains seem to offer the same effect; they also disguise the connection point of the hands to the mouth, which was a bit clunky looking. The river-like chain will give a better flow to everything.

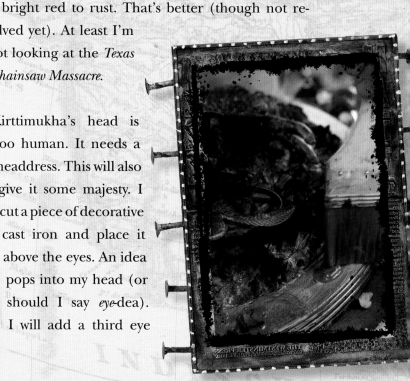

Coloration will be difficult. I decide to try something that I know from the onset won't work. I decide to try a vibrant red on the piece. Nothing says ogre like red and orange. I take a wide brush and go crazy with some Naphthol Red Light. Just as I suspected. It's a no-go. Now this really does look serial-killer-esque—bloody mouth, face and hands. I throw some Quinacridone Gold over it to at least turn the bright red to rust. That's better (though not resolved yet). At least I'm not looking at the *Texas Chainsaw Massacre*.

Kirttimukha's head is too human. It needs a headdress. This will also give it some majesty. I cut a piece of decorative cast iron and place it above the eyes. An idea pops into my head (or should I say *eye*-dea). I will add a third eye to the ogre. What a very Hindu thing to do. The opera glasses offer some of the solution. Before I attached them, I removed the mother-of-pearl eyepieces. No point of leaving them on. I grab one from my lens pile, slip an image of an eye behind the small lens and attach it with some glue.

This certifies that the fire equipment was serviceable condition on the date noted.

sometimes you should pay the piper long before you think you need to, or you'll end up paying him ten times the amount.

Well, such is the case here. I was in Lisbon and came across an amazing flea market (or whatever they call it in Portuguese). It was great. I should have bought everything I saw. It was cheap, cheap, cheap. I remember seeing booths filled with the most amazing cigar labels, some metal, most paper, but I should have purchased boxes and boxes. There was also a great booth filled with optics, such as glasses, lenses and, yes, opera glasses.

The opera glasses were wonderful—beautifully engraved, with lots of little ornaments, perfect for deconstruction. Not to mention the lenses. Everything was so cheap. I don't know if it was the exchange rate or that the items were so common. I could have bought and bought and bought.
Here's the dilemma:

43

It's about midnight, and I'm thinking I will try a bit of blue on the monster. Not all of it, just the upper two thirds. The blue I choose is Ultramarine with Titanium White and a dab of Dioxazine Purple. By George, I think I got it. The color now gives the symbolic impression of a dualistic split. The mind and the soul on the top, connected yet separate from the animal instincts of the mouth below.

Time to add the eye images to the opera glasses. Finding the right eyes is easy . . . this time (I opt for blue to go with the paint treatment). What is difficult this time around is their angle. If the inner parts point down, they look too devious; if they point up, they are too sad. Millimeters make all the difference in the world when it comes to nailing down the right expression. I'm looking for a flat emotion. I want a look that guards in front of Buckingham Palace have. No emotion, a just-the-facts-ma'am kind of look. After all, Kirttimukha is a monster just doing a job. No right. No wrong. It is what it is. After some time, I find the right position.

It's late, and I hate trying to ascertain if a piece is finished or not at such an hour. I'll have to wait till morning to know. The other reason I need to get away from the piece till morning is that I need a fresh opinion. I need Morning deMeng. You see, I find that my mind is most clear in the very wee hours of the morning. The sun isn't out yet. Nobody is really up. It is an amazingly

quiet time of the day. By far, I can get more substantial work done at this time than any other time of day. The diffi-

culty is waking up at that time. The worst time of day is in the afternoon. I think I relate that time of day with getting out of class. Hooray, it's time to play!

So I'll get some sleep and try to figure it all out in the morning. 5 a.m.? We'll see . . .

It was the beginning of the trip and I had three more weeks of wandering to go. The last thing in the world I was about to do was load up my suitcase now. In hindsight, I should have, because the opera glasses were about five bucks.

Fast forward a few years, and guess what I need? Opera glasses. I immediately remember the plethora of bargain optics in Portugal. Well, now I'm forced to wander the aisles of the Internet, in particular, eBay. There was a variety of opera glasses to choose from, none nearly as nice as what I saw in the Lisbon flea market, but I put my opening bid in at $10. It didn't take long for me to be outbid. I entered a higher amount. Outbid again. Who in the world wants opera glasses? I wonder. I bid again, and this goes on and on. Finally, I get those stupid opera glasses for thirty-two bucks. Oh, and add another eight for shipping. As the old adage goes, "When in Lisbon, buy the silly glasses."

To Judy

LILITH

Everyone knows the story of Adam and Eve; you know, trees, apples, snakes . . . not to mention conveniently located fig leaves. (I don't really know how they got those things to stay in place in Eden; one would expect a bit of frolicking.) What most people don't know is the story of Adam and Lilith, Adam's first wife. Yes, I hear all the shock and amazement. Scandal! Adam had an ex? Well, according to Jewish mythology he did. It's just like an episode of *Desperate Housewives* – The Early Years.

Lilith, it has been said, was extraordinarily beautiful. She was created from dust, in the same manner as, but separate from, Adam. Lilith was very much her own person and considered herself an equal to Adam. It was this equality that led to Lilith's departure from Adam. One day, in a moment of agitation, she invoked the name of God, grew wings and flew away, leaving Adam. So what made her leave? Was Adam somehow oppressive? Was Lilith too independent to be involved in any committed relationship? Some versions of the story actually say that it was a simple quarrel of sexual positions. In my opinion, none of these options satisfy.

There are two polar views of Lilith's personality. On one end of the spectrum, you have the perspective of a male-dominated culture. That version of Lilith's personality considered anything short of female subservience as being heretical. On the opposite end is the more recent feminist version, in which she was a champion for women's rights. I am going in a subtler direction with the story that makes neither Adam nor Lilith the root cause of the separation. Let's assume that Adam loved Lilith and Lilith loved Adam. What would create a situation that would force her to leave? In my version, it was a cultural thing. A culture that demanded Adam take on the role of superiority to the female. He may not have wanted that role, but it was the role he was charged with. Lilith, on the other hand, had no choice but to leave. She was created as an equal to Adam, so how could she accept any other situation? Her frustration, I contend, was not with Adam, but with rules placed on them, as a couple, that she could not live with.

Having no place else to go, she went to the shores of the Red Sea, in a place inhabited by demons. Here, Lilith underwent a transformation. Having denounced the rules laid before her, she attempted to create a new life, which wasn't easy. Her new consorts were the demons of the region, and it was said that she had many offspring from these demons.

Meanwhile, Adam pleaded with God to please bring Lilith back. You see, Adam didn't truly understand Lilith's plight. He couldn't see that if Lilith returned, she would no longer be the Lilith that he knew. Eventually, God acquiesced to Adam's request and sent three angels—Sanvai, Sansanvai and Semanglof—to retrieve her.

The angels found Lilith and ordered her to return to Adam at once. An indignant Lilith ignored them. This angered the three, who threatened to kill one hundred of her demonic children for every day she stayed away. She was backed into a corner by forces that wanted nothing less than subservience.

Her despair had now turned to rage. In response to the angels, she spat out her own conditions. She said that, to spite God, she would seek her revenge by taking the lives of newborns and pregnant mothers.

Sanvai, Sansanvai and Semanglof could not let this go unchallenged, and they forced her to an agreement. If she came across an amulet bearing the names of the three angels, she must spare the child. These amulets would hang above the crib in the newborn's bedroom, and they are still used to this day. In addition to the three inscribed names, they also often contain an image of a chamsah, a hand with an eye in the palm, to ward off the evil eye.

When the angels returned without Lilith, God had no choice but to create a mate for Adam that was more compatible. God was angered by Lilith's defiance, and as promised, the angels killed one hundred of her children daily. As further punishment, He instilled in her the drive to murder her own offspring every time she came across a child who was protected by the amulet. But, this didn't stop Lilith from enacting her revenge; in fact, it emboldened it. Her anger was far too profound.

Lilith is a great character study. At first, she is the heroine, an independent woman, who is in many ways a symbol for female empowerment in a world dominated by males. In this regard, she can be seen as a metaphor for revolution. Through her, the established dogma and traditional view is challenged. She is willing to risk all for her beliefs, no matter how severe the consequences.

Idealistically, this is how I envision the role of the artist. A visionary who shatters the shackles of the past to offer the revelations of a new, exciting future. In Lilith's case, she offers a new perspective, but as everyone knows, change is often greeted with fear and cynicism, and often, as in the story, violence.

In my opinion, to be considered a true Artist with a capital "A," one must challenge the accepted norm and bring new ideas to light. Repetition of the safe and customary is not the Artist's role. Art is about explorations into the unknown. This is a dangerous job because often the ideas that are brought to light are considered heretical. Many an Artist has seen the inside of a jail cell (or worse) by bringing "dangerous" thoughts to light. Lilith is such an Artist in my view because she is willing to defy the establishment (the ultimate establishment!) for her convictions.

Now, what is one to think of her reign of terror? When I first read the tale of Lilith, I was a little disturbed by her transition from role model to villain. One could attribute this to the fact that the storytellers were male, and the biases were quite visible.

Another way to look at the transformation is to view the story as a cautionary tale to all revolutionaries and extremists. Lilith began as an equal, but ultimately gave herself a position of subversive power. Ideas that could have been applied to the general good instead became personal and selfish. Anger consumed her. Historically, it is not uncommon to see revolutionary minds, once pure and idealistic, eventually become corrupted with power and spite. Creative thinkers must always evaluate and question rules, even if (especially if) the rules are ones that they themselves have created. It is a strange job of destroying fortresses, building them up, and being willing to destroy them again.

THE X

Lilith is one of those strange personas that is supposed to be a villain, but at the same time, you can't help but be moved by her tale. She is one of those dangerously seductive characters who is hard to resist. The question I'm pondering is whether I want to focus on the

story or the woman. The only thing I know for sure is that I want to include a hand with an eye somewhere in the piece. I have that aluminum latex glove mold that would be perfect for the chamsah. So I start with that. I have to decide whether the hand is up or down. I'm thinking down, and I could have it coming out of something. I'll have it come out of a shrine shape. In fact, I have a timer I just picked up at the

scrap yard. It has a nice rounded top and a dial with the hours of the day listed and then divided into day and night. I think I'll keep the night portion more prominent.

As it turns out, the hand will fit perfectly inside the timer if I do two things. First, I need to cut two little pieces of metal off the base of the hand—a couple of quick whirls of the Dremel. Done. Second, I need to cut a hole in the bottom of the timer for the hand to slide into—four whirls of the Dremel. Done.

GLOVE MOLD— *Sometimes youre looking for something in particular and you come across something even more amazing. I was working on a series of large, human-sized totems and was attempting to find some sturdy hand forms. Mannequin hands might have worked, but they would have to be just the right type. So I start my eBay search for hands. A wide array of typical, delicately gestured female hands appears. Not really what I was looking for. I needed something masculine.*

After I searched for a bit, I came across an interesting listing with no photo, "12 Latex glove molds." I thought this sounded interesting. After all, latex gloves are definitely unisex, if not downright manly. So I bid and got the batch. A week later, a crate appeared from South Carolina. I was dumbfounded. I couldnt wait to see what I had gotten myself into. Preparing myself for the worst (Ive been disappointed by my impulsive buys in the past), I cracked the crate open, and what I saw was "way cool." Inside the box were

49

The hand doesn't quite fit into the hole I cut, but it is so close. A more patient man would take the Dremel out again and widen the area; however, I am not a more patient man. I take a hammer and start pounding it in. Bam bam bam! It sometimes feels good to let out a little angst.

I have a cast-iron . . . well . . . I'm not really sure what it is, but it's a big, round, ornate thing that has some decorative function. It looks kind of compass-y, with a circle in the center and four points. I trim off three of the points, leaving the North position intact. A couple of screws and I position this behind the timer.

Since the aluminum hand is going to be the chamsah, it needs an eye; fortunately, I have many lying about. Then I need a lens. In my pile of thingies, I find a great one. It is actually something I started to use in some other piece that never got finished, but what I did was take a very large lens and mount it into some large, hollow gear from the auto salvage yard. I am sure there is a specific name for the item, but I'm not a car guy. (As a sidenote, I did try to become a car guy. I purchased a black '63 Mercury Monterey that looked like the Batmobile. Quite a fun ride, but I had to decide if I wanted to make art or spend all my money and time fixing a car. I think you can guess what my decision was.) In any event, it made for a very nice and very heavy frame for the lens. A little Liquid Nails and the hand is ready to ward off the evil eye.

I am looking for an image of Adam; it doesn't need to actually be *the* Adam, it just needs to be a full body shot of a man. The magazines have plenty of male images,

two rows of metal hands mounted upright on a metal base. The hands weren't exactly life-like; rather, they were downright simple looking. In fact, they reminded me of a robot hand from a 1950s sci-fi movie.

It took me a while to figure out how they made gloves from these forms, but as I was fiddling with them I realized that on some of the hands there was still a thin, clear coating of latex. I peeled it off and voila, a glove. It appears that the latex is poured over these upright forms and then dried, and gloves are born. Nifty. Periodically, I will search for these, but I have never seen them again. Someday I will find another batch, and all will be right in the world (or left, depending on your handedness).

METAL SCRAP YARD

TIMER— I recently received an e-mail in which someone had asked whether I had a day job working at a post-apocalyptic amusement park. How cool would that be? (Not the working, but the designing.) I envision rides like the Nuclear Submarine (complete

but none of them is the pose I am looking for. Maybe an anatomical drawing? I am reminded of the TV series *The Time Tunnel*, where the opening credits had a silhouette of a man falling down a tunnel. It was cartoon-like but had a construction-paper-cutout quality. It was a popular graphic image in the late 1950s and early 1960s; in fact, I think they used a similar image in the *Vertigo* movie poster. I decide to give this style a try, and I cut a man out of white paper.

Sitting on my workbench under piles of paper, I find an opera glasses case. At first I think I'll try floating the silhouette inside of the case. I play around with this option for a bit, but don't commit just yet.

A winged image of Isis happens my way, and I play with the idea of using this form and replacing the face with something different. I attach it at the top of the timer. It looks okay, I guess. The problem I am having is the piece is too subtle. I want this work to be powerful, and I want Lilith to be more prominent.

I wander into my house and grab a cup of coffee. This must have been my thirty-seventh cup for the day, which would explain why I've had to use the bathroom so many times. Each time I used the toilet, I would notice a magazine. This time I focus on the cover featuring a woman wearing a burka. Her eyes are beautiful and mysterious. I relax in my living room drinking my coffee, and I start to notice my mask collection. I have a number of them from various cultures. A light bulb goes on. I grab the magazine and go out to the studio, splashing coffee along the way.

with mutant sea monsters), *It's a Fall-Out World After All*, and the *Haunted Bomb Shelter*. Well, we all have our dreams.

The closest thing to such a theme park is the local metal scrap yard. What amazing places these can be. I love wandering through the mounds of rust and metal, and strolling through the valleys of crushed cars. A tenuous feeling, to be sure. One never knows when a piece of metal might shift and come tumbling down, especially when you're like me and you're busy yanking on objects at the base of these jumbled steel mountains. If the crushing tons of metal don't get you, there is always the potential of laceration from sharp, pointy things . . . oh, and let's not forget tetanus. Very exciting really.

One day, I was perusing for goodies, treading through the oily mud. In one hand was a large bucket of heavy gears, which was so heavy, in fact, I thought for sure that the handle would snap. This did not happen, but I did find myself continuously switching hands

My bright idea is to transform this into something part shrine, part mask. I cut the brown eyes out of the magazine and, replacing the Adam figure, I insert them into the case for opera glasses. This completely alters the piece. Suddenly, the timer becomes some exotic headdress. This allows me to play with some new ideas. I can use the timer as an area that implies the thoughts of Lilith; it would be like looking into her psyche.

From my pile of junk, I pull out a metal plate that had been used for printing books. It has some interesting designs on it, so it gets positioned inside the headdress to use as a background for the cutout Adam.

A wash of Quinacridone Gold is painted over most of the piece. As usual, I never know if it will work out, but it is my favorite base color. It just works so well beneath so many other colors. I try a wash of purple over the Quinacridone Gold. Sometimes this gives a nice reddish rust quality. In this case, it doesn't really do much for me, but I leave it for the time being.

I decide to cover the eyes slightly with a tiny grid. Lilith is now looking through a barrier. She is exiled.

Despite what mothers might say, matches are fun to play with. Through my experiences with Liquid Nails, however, I have learned that one has to be a bit cautious using flames around the stuff when it isn't dry. It has a gasoline-like vapor that can create quite a bit of excitement. Such a situation just happened. I

to relieve the strain on my arms.
I would imagine that what a chef
experiences wandering through
an outdoor market is what I
experience mucking through the
metal heaps. In one pile, beautiful
silver coils of metal borings. In
another, rusted radiators. All
the while, a crane magnet swept
by overhead (sometimes a bit too
close for comfort).

I wandered through a section
that is typically ignored by
welders—what I call the "impure
area". Devices that contain a
variety of materials abound.
At some point, through some
process unknown to me, the metal
is somehow separated from all
plastic and rubber. The reason
I like this area is that it is
great pickin's for plastic dials,
speedometers—the type of stuff
that really would be recycled as-is
and certainly wouldn't survive the
de-plastification process.

Like the Holy Grail, it appeared
to me. On top of a mound of
dishwasher parts sat this little
electrical timer from decades past.
It was perched like a shrine atop
a mountain. In fact, it looked a
bit contrived. Almost as if it

55

was using some matches on a bit of paper I had glued down, and next thing I know, whoosh (the same "whoosh" that comes from igniting the pilot light in the stove). Suddenly, the entire piece has a butane-blue glow to it. This isn't the first time this has happened to me, so I know I have at least a moment to extinguish the flames before they start to do some damage. A few quick puffs of air and the fire is out. Yes, I do have a fire extinguisher handy when I do this sort of thing.

A greenish-blue coat of paint is placed over the Quinacridone Gold. Much, much better. I associate this color with the Middle East, for some reason (especially when combined with a purple). Sometimes adding an unexpected bit of color can draw attention to areas that are being overlooked. I place a red dot in the center of the eye/hand. After I do this, I decide that the color seems a bit lonely there, and I add the same color in the upper region, in the center of the timer. The viewer will notice the top dot and immediately be drawn to the lower red, thus moving his gaze through the piece of art. This is my theory, anyway.

A wire here and dab of paint there and I think I have my Lilith shrine/mask. For me, it has this feeling of Lilith being haunted by her past. Her life with Adam, forever inside her mind, forever reminding her of her banishment.

had been placed there, in this arrangement, intentionally. Perhaps. Perhaps not. In my business of looking for found objects, I have come to learn that the haphazard can strangely create order. Just look at my work if you don't believe me. Or better yet, just look at my studio.

A NOTE ON THE CHAMSAH

Literally translated as "hand," chamsah means "five" in Hebrew; the hand has five digits, and each digit represents the five names of God that are represented in different ways in the Jewish Bible. Those five names combined are a very powerful source of warding off evil. The chamsah is a symbol that has fascinated me for years. Before I knew its specific meaning, I developed my own metaphor for this image. I envisioned it as a connection from the divine (the eye) to the physical plane (the hand). For me, it symbolized the artist seeing through his/her hands, bringing divinity to the world through art. Ultimately, the goal is the same: to bring the divine into the world as a means of serving humanity. Isn't that also the purpose of art?

57

CAT. N°. P224C sys
COIL RES. 256 OHMS

REMOVE THIS PLATE
AND RENEW DRY CELLS
EVERY SIX MONTHS OR
WHEN INSTRUMENT LACKS
SENSITIVITY. INSERT NEW
CELLS SO THAT CENTER
TERMINAL OF CELL
MAKES CONTACT
WITH THIS PLATE

To my niece, the little artist

Maddy

MORPHEUS

Deep in the underworld of Greek mythology, there is a cave on the isle of Lemnos. At its entryway, along with other sleep-inducing plants, grow wild poppies. Not an easy place to enter without falling spell to its inhabitant, Hypnos, god of sleep. Inside, it is entirely devoid of sunlight, and here Hypnos rests on a large couch, comfortable, as one might imagine the god of sleep to be. Through his chamber, the river Lethe flows; one sip of its waters and all is forgotten.

Hypnos was son of the goddess of night, Nyx. Hypnos's three most prominent sons were called the Oneiroi: Phobetor, Phantasos and Morpheus; the gods of dreams. Phobetor was in charge of nightmares, as well as creating the illusions of animals. Phantasos was in charge of strange, fantastical scenes, as well as replicating inanimate objects. Morpheus had a special talent in that he could mimic any human. He could replicate not only their look, but also their mood, voice and, occasionally, touch.

The story begins with a king and queen (like many stories do). King Ceyx was heading off on a long sea voyage; his wife, Halcyone, heartbroken and perhaps sensing tragedy, pleaded with her lover to stay. Tempted but not swayed, Ceyx departed, promising his return within two cycles of the moon.

A great storm befell the ship. Lightning shattered the mast. Waves ripped the wood from the vessel's side. All the crew was left swimming, and eventually drowned in the violent sea. But before Ceyx drifted below the watery surface he uttered the name of his beloved wife, "Halcyone," hoping that she might hear of his fate. Then he was gone.

Meanwhile, unaware of her husband's tragedy, Halcyone made an offering every day to the goddess Hera for his safe return. This saddened Hera, for she was aware of Ceyx's demise, and it was a bit awkward to receive prayers for the safe return of a dead man. So Hera sent a message to Hypnos to send Morpheus on an important journey.

Morpheus flew from his cave to Halcyone's bedside and began transforming. He removed his wings and began to take on the appearance of the drowned king—his mannerisms, his voice and his look. But his image was not of the king as he looked when he was alive, but that of a dead man. His skin was pale, and his features gaunt. His hair and beard dripped with saltwater as he stood before her. At first, Halcyone didn't recognize her lover, but it was not because Morpheus's imitation was faulty. Rather, it was because it was too accurate; Halcyone had never seen her husband in such an anguished state.

Morpheus leaned over the bed, tears streaming from his eyes, and said, "Do you recognize me? Or has death changed me too much?" Halcyone then realized that it was her husband that stood before her. Morpheus, being a master of impression, told her Ceyx's sad tale, as Ceyx himself would have relayed it, and said, "Pray for me no more; I am dead. Instead, mourn for me." With that, Morpheus flew off.

Halcyone awoke, now aware of the horrid truth. She headed for the shore where she last saw her husband before he met his doom. She noticed a large form floating. Not certain what it could be, she waded in to get closer. As she approached it, she could tell that it was a human. She waded in even farther, and as she did, the body seemed to drift toward her. It was Ceyx. He had kept his vow and returned to his wife, alas, lifeless. She embraced him and wept.

Mad with despair, she climbed a large stone pier as the gods watched. Looking down at the rocky reef beneath her, Halcyone jumped. The gods, feeling such sadness, quickly intervened, and Halcyone's arms suddenly became wings. It was as if she had been a bird all her life; she swooped and hovered until she got a glimpse of Ceyx's body in the sea. Flying toward him, she called out in her new bird voice. At first, there was no response; then Ceyx magically transformed into a bird. He flew up to his love, and they flew off together.

Meanwhile, Morpheus reclined on his ebony bed and relaxed after his very emotionally exhausting performance. He was the first method actor, and he actually felt the pain from his portrayals, which is what made him so good at what he did. Even so, he needed a drink; or maybe those poppies came in handy.

Birds of a feather flock . . . no, that's not what I want to talk about. What I want to talk about is Morpheus, the master of dreams (artists love dreams), and the concept of an artist as someone who reproduces reality.

The concept of realism is an interesting topic. What exactly is reality? During the Classical Period in ancient Greece, beautiful bodies of gods, goddesses, men and women filled the cities. Some would say that this was realism. Was it? I wish that what I saw in the mirror looked as good as those gods and heroes. This wasn't realism; rather, it was idealism.

Compare idealism to the art of the Dutch painters of the 1600s. Their approach was certainly very realistic, in a sense. Everyday scenes, in many cases. Still lifes that really capture the nature of the object. But was it realism?

Realism is a strange thing, because artists, no matter how hard they try not to, will always inject a little bit of themselves into a piece of art. It's quite easy to tell a Vermeer from a Rembrandt, even when they paint a similar subject. The lighting Vermeer preferred for his scenes (sort of an early-morning glow) is on the opposite side of the spectrum from Rembrandt (who seemed to prefer something that was a bit more candlelit). Reality is subjective. Imagine a car that has the driver's side painted red and the passenger's side painted blue; the side of the street you're standing on is going to change the car's reality for you.

So, what about artists like myself who don't create directly from nature? If something is a creation of my mind, is this not realism? I see a reality that may not be a depiction of the shared outside world, but rather an attempt to find a reality from a secret world.

So what sort of an artist was Morpheus? Classical? Renaissance? Expressionist? I think in order for someone to do a job like his, he would have to be all of the art forms of the world combined. He would have to become not only the physical person, but also the soul of the person. He would have to become all the ideas that come to mind when that person is thought about.

A difficult job Morpheus has, and one shouldn't merely think of him as an impressionist. He becomes the person based on the perspective of the viewer. He's one kick-butt artist.

DREAM BOX

Morpheus is cool. Of all the Greek gods, he is my favorite and, actually, one of the most obscure. I love to envision him flying from dream to dream and transforming his physical appearance. Plus, even his name is hip. When I envision him, I think of him preparing for his various dream roles inside of a stereotypical opium den, lush with deep red colors and lit by gaslight. This is what makes me think that I really want to do a piece where I can incorporate lighting. If done properly, it can really create the mood of mys-

This certifies that the fire equipment was serviceable condition on the date noted.

THE STUDIO

FOOTLOCKER— Sure, Art is sacred, especially when it's spelled with a capital "A". However, I have a little secret to confess: As long as it is still in my studio, nothing is sacred. While I'm working on certain projects, I get to an impasse. A piece of art is just not working, so this is typically when I start grabbing junk and images or whatever, to see if some fresh object might help out the dilemma. Sometimes what I end up grabbing is artwork on the wall. I start dissecting it and using its parts in other pieces. It's true. Typically, it is only done with artworks that I am not entirely satisfied with. If I don't love it, it's subject to being devoured by some other work of art.

One question I get all the time is, "Don't you hate seeing your work leave your possession when it's sold?" Absolutely not! At least when it's sold it's safe from me. Every day that a piece is in my domain, the chance that it will be absorbed into something else greatly increases.

tery that is indicative of his reputation.

My studio is filled with old suitcases and typewriter cases. I have plenty of stuff that I could use for a lightbox. Sometimes, however, it is easier to grab an artwork off the wall that I never felt was truly resolved. In this case I choose a light fixture I created in an old footlocker.

So I get down to basics. First I need to attack the light fixture. I have to begin there because when I work this way (creating a piece that lights up), I want to work from the inside out. I want the inside image to decide what happens on the outside of the box. The footlocker already has a hole in

the front from past incarnations; this will be where the viewer looks in. I can already tell that some sort of lens will have to go over this opening.

The light is in place and I must figure out what in the world will be illuminated inside. I want it to be as if the viewer is peering into the god's underworld parlor of illusions. I happen to have some images I photocopied onto transparencies. In particular, I have an image of a man with his eyes closed with a somewhat meditative look. I apply the transparency to a piece of paper that I painted in reds and fireplace yellows. The clear photocopy has a ghostly effect. It needs some substantiality to it, however, so I decide to also add a tangible heart image over his chest. The heart may not go with the myth, but it looks good. I suppose I could say that Morpheus empathized with Ceyx and Halcyone . . . with all his heart. But that's a stretch.

For me to really hone this image down, I need to know what the viewer is going to be peering through. I need to know what sort of lens magnification will be taking place.

I buy new watches all the time. Not for artwork, but because I just get bored wearing the same watch all of the time and I have to move on to something new. Perhaps my real motive for going through so many watches is that I just want to use them in art. I have this one watch that has been sitting around for a while. I try it out over the hole, but the lens doesn't quite work with the interior images.

Too much of the parlor scene is visible, not to mention the light bulb and the wires. If the magnification is higher, the structural stuff will be indiscernible. Easy enough: pop out the crystal that came with the watch and sort

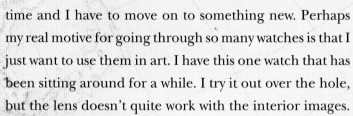

This is exactly what happened with the footlocker. It was given to me outside a bar. Someone I knew had been saving it for me, and the art exchange was made. I immediately turned it into a lightbox thing. If I recall, it was pretty nifty. A very simple design: a painted box with some adornments and a flicker flame peeking through a large lens. Time wore on. Certain things about the piece annoyed me more and more. It was too blue. It was too trite. That sort of stuff.

While I was working on a different piece, a smaller piece that incorporated an iron, I decided that I need the iron to be housed in something. I looked around, and there was that annoying lightbox. I wasted no time and started dissecting the box so that the iron would fit. When all was said and done, it was a nice piece . . . for a while.

Once again, the day came when it annoyed me once more, hopefully for the final time. This time, it made it into the Morpheus piece. Finally, I think the work is safe from my dismembering hand. For starters, it turned out to be much

63

through my large and very coveted collection of optics. I try a few and find one that will do the trick nicely.

A large metal circle thing will surround the lens. It weighs a ton, so I need to add loads of Liquid Nails to hold it in place. This gives me an idea. A nice effect might be filling the interior of this metal ring with a random jumble of doodads or the like. I opt for nails; after all, if one is peering into the underworld, it must be a bit treacherous. I grab my caulk gun and goop up the space between the metal and the lens. Then, I start plopping nails in the area. I keep the arrangement random.

I'm still a bit indecisive about the exterior of the box. That familiar feeling of frustration is creeping in. Fortunately for me it is *Seinfeld* time. I am a total *Seinfeld* addict. I've seen every episode over a bajillion times, and I still find them hilarious. So, I sit down to clear my mind for a stretch. By the way, it is the episode where Kramer makes a pasta sculpture of Jerry—Fusilli Jerry.

All is well. My mind has had its dose of *Seinfeld* zen-ification and I can jump back into painting. So far, so good. I like the warm reds that are going on. I need to alter the nails so they're no longer silver. A few washes of Quinacridone Gold, a a light wash of Naphthol Red Light and . . . voilà—rusty. I then add a wave design—nothing fancy, just the repeti-

more resolved than its previous incarnations. Secondly, it is safe in the hands of my editor. I have a feeling she may not send it back after she reads this section.

GARAGE SALE

OLD NAILS— *Garage sales are hit or miss. I love going to garage sales, but there is another part of me that absolutely hates it. What I hate is trying to figure out which ones are the good ones before you invest your time traveling to a location. Sometimes you can figure it out by the location, other times your instincts are all wrong. I hate nothing more than driving up and seeing baby toys and baby clothes. In this case, the lawn is usually strewn with broken toys, all in the colors of red, yellow and blue. What a horrible sight, and yes, it is true that I am not a fan of Piet Mondrian's artwork because of this very association.*

One time, I was scanning the paper for garage sales, and I noticed a less-than-desirable location. It's not that it was in a bad area, but it was in an area that, in my experience, was renowned for its secondhand

tive W-pattern that you see in cartoons to represent water. This is the river that runs through the cave of Hypnos and his sons.

One problem I am seeing is that, even with the sea design on the box, the area around the lens is pretty vacant. I'm not sure why the idea came to me, but I'm thinking I'll pound a bunch of thin nails into those boring areas and then glue tiny squares of numbers (from book pages) onto each head.

I do this and I notice that it reminds me of something I've seen in movies or art—little words or objects fluttering surrealistically around someone's head. It creates a nice visual layer to look through and definitely adds intrigue to the once empty spaces.

Once upon a time, I used palm tree images frequently. I really don't know why I was drawn to them. Maybe it was because they have such a simple yet recognizable form. Under my work area, I have a drawer filled with palm tree photocopies. I find a couple of trees that were taken from an old Columbian-era map. (I really dig the maps of the 1600s with all the ornate designs and crazy sea monsters lurking about.) I mount the tree images onto a couple of pieces of wood and glue them on either side of the lens area. I notice in the same pile of scrap papers the periodic table abbreviations. Just for kicks I randomly pick a couple elements and glue them to the back of lenses; I then attach them to the base of the trees. They don't really have anything to do with anything, but they look good. As I write this, I am reminded of all the times that I randomly add items to a piece, seemingly with no meaning. Months pass, sometimes even years. And then one day, something dawns on me. That random, pointless addition is actually incredibly pertinent. I just didn't see the significance. Truth is that I probably do know what I'm do-ing when I add these types of items, but I only know it subcon-sciously. I'll be curi-ous if these trees with periodic letters hit me with a lightning bolt of awareness at some point in the future. I'll let you know.

toddler toys. I wasn't even going to consider it. But I was already in the neighborhood. I thought I should at least stop in. (How many times had I said this and been disappointed?)

So I pulled up in the driveway. No primary colors anywhere! Whew. The place had tons of old hardware and power tools. In the garage, there was a wall of shelves that was completely filled with hundreds of Sanka, Skippy, and Gerber jars. Each of these jars was labeled and contained something different. Some contained door fixtures. Some contained brass tacks. Some contained copper rivets. Most of the jars contained various types of screws or nails. How tantalizing!

What was truly amazing about this display was that the objects inside the jars had been used and then saved so as not to waste even the most inexpensive nail or bolt. One had to be impressed by the person's frugality. I got the impression that this was someone who had lived through tough financial times, perhaps

Piling through old bins of machine parts, I find handfuls of goodies that might work out. As usual, I need more stuff. I like to tell people that I'm not a minimalist, I'm a maximalist. Some say, "Less is more." I say, "More is the new less." I truly believe this . . . more or less.

Now I'm really getting somewhere—a thingy here, a god-knows-what there. I then find something cool: a metal bird that was either a hood ornament or a trophy ornament. The wings that Morpheus flew in on, or it could represent the birds that Ceyx and Halcyone changed into.

I want to make the box look more electrical, as a way of visually playing off the interior light. So I run some copper wires around the frame surrounding the box. It's kind of a fun trick to play. Making people think that objects with visual function are actually serving some utilitarian task. Trickery and illusion, that's the name of the game.

Uh . . . I realize, as I add a few more washes of paint to the whole thing, I have the light on and plugged in. Not really a good idea to have water dripping down into light sockets. The problem is that I get so caught up in the work, sometimes I start ignoring certain life-endangering situations. Nobody could ever say I don't risk my life for art, and by the looks of the final project, it is well worth the risk of electrocution. Kids, please don't try this at home.

the Depression, and refused to squander belongings, no matter how seemingly insignificant.

None of the jars were priced so I asked the woman running the sale, and she responded, "Free." "Wow," I replied, or maybe I said, "Holy Toledo." Either way, I told her I would take the whole wall. She was ecstatic. Apparently, her husband had passed on, and this was his little fetish. She was moving, and what in the world would she do with Sanka jars filled with used cabinet hinges and roofing nails?

She helped me load up my van, and off I drove, the sound of glass jars melodically rattling as I tried to figure out how I was going to make room in the studio for all of this stuff.

Once in a while, when I use an object from one of those jars, I wonder what that man would have thought of me using these items in ways they were never intended to be used. I sometimes imagine him wincing as I use his rusty nails as adornments for a work of art, as opposed to nailing shingles down. Then again, he would probably just be happy to see they are being put to use. 69

To Georgia

ORPHEUS AND EURYDICE

Orpheus was a master musician and poet who was so gifted that when he played, wild beasts were charmed, trees and rocks could be coaxed into dance, and rivers ceased to flow so that they could listen to his song. Now *that's* an artist. This is a romantic (albeit tragic) tale of one artist's love—his love for that thing nearest and dearest to his soul, his wife, Eurydice.

It begins with Eurydice fleeing from the god Aristaeus. (One can only imagine his intentions; after all, Greek gods were not exactly known for their ethical behavior.) Entering a field of tall grass, she felt something sharp on her bare foot. She looked down to see a venomous snake with its fangs embedded in her skin. As quickly as she saw it, it slithered away, and poison moved quickly through her veins. She collapsed into the cool green and her world went dark.

When Orpheus found her, there was no sign of life. Eurydice had been given a one-way ticket to the underworld, land of Hades. Overcome with grief, Orpheus took to his lyre and began to play. As he sang of his lost love, all the world's creations froze, mesmerized with his tale of woe. Even the gods were moved and whispered advice in his ear.

A dangerous journey now before him, Orpheus set out to find Eurydice. His first stop: the river Styx and the grim ferryman whose task was to transport the souls of the newly departed across the river to the gates of Hades. Of course, when the ferryman saw Orpheus, a living man, he refused him entry into his boat. But it's amazing what a little music can do; all it took was a song. The two crossed the dark river and, not being much of a conversationalist, the ferryman was content to listen to the magic that emanated from the mouth of a living man.

On the opposite shore, Orpheus stepped from the boat to encounter a large gate. In front of it stood a chomping, snarling, three-headed dog, Cerberus. It has been said that Orpheus was really more of cat person than a dog person; even so, this was a bit extreme for a guard dog. Orpheus retrieved lyre and sang his sad song. Cerberus succumbed to the verses of Orpheus, and the gates swung open.

When he reached the throne of Hades, Orpheus stated his desire to retrieve Eurydice and bring her back to the surface, to the land of the sun. Now, mere tales of woe did not easily move Hades; he had heard them all before.

Orpheus moved his fingers across the strings of his lyre and once again began his song. At first, his voice trembled in the presence of such a powerful deity, but it soon smoothed with the thought of his precious Eurydice. The tune echoed through the tunnels of the underworld and even the diamonds, hidden in their black obsidian rocks, sparkled from the music, creating starlight in the cavernous domain.

Hades trembled at this young man's beautiful gift, and he wept tears of iron. So touched was he by this unique mortal, he agreed to Orpheus's plea, but with a string attached. On their journey back to the land of light, Orpheus would walk in front of Eurydice and never look back at her until they reached the surface. Simple enough (so it seemed). Without hesitancy, he agreed and prepared for the return trip.

The return trip seemed to take twice as long. The tunnel out was dark and silent. Not even his own footsteps could Orpheus hear, let alone the footsteps of his wife. He called her name, "Eurydice?" Silence. Up ahead, the light of the world above could be seen, but still no response from Eurydice. Orpheus wondered if Hades had betrayed him. Was she there behind him? He sensed she was, but couldn't be sure. So much silence and darkness; the absence of senses overwhelmed him and he forgot his pact with Hades. He turned. . .

What he saw was a glimpse, a shadow of the woman he loved, falling away from him, back to the shadows, back to the dark caves of Hades. As Eurydice fell, the gates to the underworld closed, barring Orpheus from reentry. Eurydice was lost. All that remained was her memory and her song, which Orpheus sang until the day he would be reunited with her in the land of the dead.

This story is, in many ways, the story of the typical assemblage artist. It is the story of seeking out precious things in the most undesirable of places. I think of the time I spend wandering around scrap yards surrounded by razor-sharp objects, oil and goo. It's hard not to think of tetanus wandering down these halls of cars and refrigerators, my shoes covered in inches of a muddy muck. Have I not crossed the river Styx? Eurydice has got to be in here somewhere, but what form will she take—a gear, a strange copper device, perhaps an old telephone? I'll know it when I see it. This process of searching through objects that once had value but through time have been banished to the land of dust and rust is not so different from the story of Orpheus. He too had the task of breaking the barrier between past and present, and then bringing new life to something precious, once lost.

Using this metaphor, I see Eurydice as the strange, enigmatic summons that all artists experience. She is the muse that entices one to find something dear and precious. To find her, one must enter a nebulous place: the land of dreams and intuition. Here is the source of all creation—the cosmic womb, a place without form but from which all things are formed. No creative idea is born without this essential journey inward.

Orpheus, the artist, used all his skills to retrieve his Eurydice, to summon her to the surface and make her tangible again. The irony is, of course, that to do this, he had to abandon all five of his senses. He would have to trust only his heart. Not so far off from a typical day in the art studio, really. As for the journey, it is often as difficult as anything that Orpheus had to face.

Of course, in the end, Orpheus loses Eurydice. Oh, how many times has this happened to me? A glimpse of perfection, a work of art so close to reaching the high water mark, and then—lost. Sometimes a glimpse is all I get, and then it's back to the easel, back to the paint, back to the three-headed dogs. Such is the bane and blessing of all creative people: the endless search. The curse of Orpheus is that he could descend only once. Fortunately for the artist, the journey inward can continue as long as the heart beats and long as there is passion in the soul.

DOWN TO EARTH

I'm in need of just the right object to initiate a work inspired by Orpheus and Eurydice. I try a fancy cast-iron wall hanging, but it doesn't fit the theme. Next option: the small cabinet I found at a garage sale. Actually, it's perfect. It's divided into top and bottom compartments—"upper" and "lower" to signify the division between the underworld and the earth. So what to add to it? I try placing a variety of thingamajigs on and around the cabinet to gauge how they would visually work with each other. I pick up the fancy cast-iron piece again and place it behind, in front . . . anywhere? No, too busy, but the *cast-iron* gives me another idea. What happened to that bag of stove parts that I found in the

woods? Last I saw it, it was under those three encyclopedia volumes . . . still there. I take the pieces from the bag and try them out in various locations on the cabinet. I decide the long skirt pieces belong at the top and bottom, while the decorative floral plate can be attached on top of the upper skirt. So far, so good.

I want the lower compartment to suggest either the descent or Eurydice falling back to Hades, but what of the upper portion? I look around some more. I pull out suitcases full of things. Too big. Too gaudy. Too this. Too that. Too the other thing. I look up onto a high shelf. There it is—the campfire toaster. Will it fit? I stumble over piles of items and pull it down from the shelf. It fits like a glove, not to mention that it creates an interesting tunnel effect that, as luck would have it, is ideal for this theme.

LOCAL BAR

CAMP TOASTER— I remember the day of revelation well; I was sitting in a local Missoula bar swilling a pint of locally brewed Old Bongwater Ale. The baseball postseason was underway and televised games surrounded me: Boston Red Sox vs. Chicago White Sox. (For a Boston fan, such as myself, the outcome looked grim.) My friend George, who is a sculptor, wanders in with a brown paper bag that has seeping oil stains. "Early Christmas presents," he says. I peek inside and find some beautiful, old, gunked-up gears that only I would appreciate. I look deeper in the bag and pull out an object. For years I had seen objects such as these in secondhand stores and had absolutely no idea what they were. They are somewhat bell-shaped, though square, and look like a cross between a cheese grater and the top of a lantern. One distinguishing feature is that they are always, always rusty. I asked George if he knew what it was, and he had absolutely no idea.

My friends John and Kathy showed up then (fashionably late as usual), and as they plopped down, Kathy said, looking at the object in my hand, "Oh, an old camp toaster." Not being much of a camper, I said I had absolutely no

73

Time to start assembling. Liquid Nails? Check. Drill with screwdriver bit? Check. Screws? Check. *Extra* tubes of Liquid Nails? Check. I opt for a glue/screw combo; better safe than sorry. A bit of glue, some wood screws, the "rrrrrrrrrr" of the drill gun—I'm totally in my element now. Everything assembles like clockwork, and the basic form is done. Now comes the challenge of choosing imagery to match the form. It's time for the encyclopedia.

I'm looking for the face of Orpheus. Maybe not literally, but a face that embodies how I envision his character—an explorer who is determined to find his lost love. Unfortunately, encyclopedias circa 1945 are not known for their photographs of heroes incarnate. They tend to focus more on bad-haired scientists. Wait, I spoke too soon; lo and behold, a statue of Constantine. Hmmm . . . I think this will work. His eyes are a bit large, but I'll worry about that later. I cut the image out, glue it onto a piece of matboard and install the floating head into the toaster tunnel.

What of Eurydice and falling? I did find a nice image of a falling woman in a graphic arts magazine, but it emphasized the wrong point. To me, Orpheus's tale is about the search and not the loss—a willingness to do anything to find what one is looking for. Eurydice is an ideal. She belongs above him, like a thought bubble floating over his head. Somewhere, I have a face that was cut out of a magazine long ago . . . and here it is. A bit of clear glue and a lens, and I place Eurydice in her new home: the center of the round floral piece of cast iron.

idea what a camp toaster was or how it worked. She explained that you lay it on a campfire, lean the bread on the four sides of the device, and voilà—toast.

Now that she had explained that, it all made sense. Some of the past life of this object was revealed, years of foggy bewilderment were lifted. Now that I knew what it was, it was time to turn it into something completely different. Oh, Boston lost 5 to 3. A bad day for baseball, a good day for found object edification.

MORNING HIKE

CAST-IRON STOVE— It's funny what you find in the middle of nowhere. I was on a walking trail that resembled more of a game trail. No pickup truck would make it this far into the woods, so someone must have brought these strange and beautiful objects here. Three decorative pieces from a cast iron stove: two identical long metal pieces that were probably the skirt, and a round piece with some lovely floral designs. Who would bring a stove to the middle of Lolo National Forest? There are no houses around anywhere—just trees, a light dust of snow, puddles of mud and pine needles. Whatever happened to the rest of the stove? A mystery I'll never be able to solve.

75

The underworld portion is bare. Perhaps some burnt dictionary pages? It is Hades, after all; everything is burnt or burning, right? I add a number of pages, and now I can turn to my paints—but wait, what's this scrap on the ground? It's a dictionary scrap showing a gear image. Awhile back, I was going to use this on another piece of art. Needless to say, I never did. I pick it up and something strange and magical happens. On the backside is an image of a man descending (or perhaps ascending) a rope ladder! This couldn't be any more auspicious. (I should mention that serendipity is no stranger to my studio.) The image must be used, and I know exactly where to put it—as if that spot had been waiting for this little scrap of paper all along.

When it's finally time to paint, my goal is to unify all the various elements, making them appear comfortable in their new environment. Many of the objects I have used have no business being together, so this is a way to ease the transition. Paint and various washes of color have the effect of making it seem as if all the various components have experienced the same conditions of time, weather, wear and tear. I start with washes of earth tones, but the hues don't quite feel right.

I try a rusty red. Too much (and maybe too violent). I ponder a moment . . . what about oceanic colors? The ocean is a strange, alien world that can elicit a feeling of things lost and irretrievable. It's not the Hades seen in comics, but the fiery route seems to hit the wrong note. I add an oxidized blue-green color. Ideal—that's it. It's amazing to me how color can completely transform a piece.

Designs, patterns and little archetypical forms are added. (Carl Jung would be proud.) They serve two functions: one, to convey a strange alchemical feel; and two, to aid in the unification of disparate shapes and forms. Alongside the magic of color, continuing a design element through a variety of objects helps meld the whole thing together.

Having no control or knowledge of the previous lives of discarded objects is what makes them magical and enigmatic. For me, objects like these stove parts have seen things that I can only imagine. Who did this stove keep warm? Who did it cook for? And more recently, what brought it to a point of dismantlement and abandonment?

SATURDAY GARAGE SALE

$2 CABINET— A rainy Saturday morning: I decided to forgo the farmer's market in favor of the garage sales. (From a buyer's standpoint, prices go way down with the slightest indication of rain.) It was my third stop. I had been following a local secondhand storeowner from place to place. I figured he knew where the good stuff was—after all, this was his livelihood. So there I was, at sale number three.

Nothing was really flipping my pancakes until I saw a huge collection of snow globes. Some had assorted state themes, some had Christmas images, some had beach scenes . . . I bought thirty (25 cents a piece). Having nothing to carry them in, I glanced around and saw a small $2 cabinet, the type of thing that you find at TJ Maxx for $8. The price was right, and I thought I might

I'm close—really on the cusp of completion, but a few things still bother me. Small things like Orpheus's big eyes. Time to pull a familiar trick from my sleeve: cutting out a rectangular strip of eyes from one image and, like a mask, placing them over the eyes of another image. I think this creates an interesting visual and psychological effect. The eyes are considered the windows to the soul, so by mismatching the eyes and face, I think it creates a feeling of strife; the inner and the outer worlds in conflict—exactly what Orpheus needed! This process of finding the right eyes is painstaking. Hours go by until I find the right eyes that relate to the face and express the emotions I desire: compassion, desperation and determination. I finally find the eyes in an issue of *National Geographic*, in an article about Latin Americans. *Bueno!*—The eyes have it.

Something inspires me to run wires across the lower portion. This adds some visual intrigue, but the top and the bottom halves still need to somehow be visually connected. Something from above needs to descend, tying the halves together—something that makes sense thematically. Thinking of the ocean theme, my mind flashes to images of long, black tendril-like coral. I turn to a pile that I very seldom look through, the pile of plastic plants slated for deportation, but I have a hunch something in this pile will work. I find an aquarium plant that is not black but has the look I need, so I paint it. Ta-da—black coral. In this position, it suggests subterranean roots, another appropriate symbol. Two for the price of one! Could this be the final touch? Am I finished? It certainly seems like it, but time will be the judge. I need a few hours of distance. I need to see it in the light of a new day. I need a martini.

The next morning, cup of coffee in hand, I walk out to the studio to see if I was deluding myself the night before. I look. It hits a chord that can't be experienced without a bit of separation. I can tell that this is a finished work. Orpheus has descended. I sit back in my couch, looking and drinking coffee. Yep, it's finished. I look around the studio mess. Okay, now what?

actually be able to create something from it someday. ("Someday" seldom comes immediately.)

SPECIAL DELIVERY

PLASTIC PLANT— On my doorstep was a small aquarium filled with various boxes and bags, but no note as to whom it was from. This was not too uncommon, since I do have a reputation as the local "trash collector". Sometimes this really means trash, sometimes treasure. This day it was a bit of both.

Inside the fish tank were things like hoses, and pumps, and rocks, and, to my dismay, plastic plants. I'm not a big fan of fake flowers, and plastic flowers are the worst. The last purge I made, I had eliminated all signs of this offensive plastic. I thought I was safe until today.

I would concede that aquarium plants are a small notch up in the artificial flora category. My dilemma: I feel a bit guilty disposing of items, no matter how unappealing or dysfunctional, when they were given to me out of kindness. So I kept the plastic plants. My philosophy? If I keep them for six months, and I still haven't incorporated them into a piece of art, I can dispose of them, and it's then their own fault. **79**

To my grandmother May

OSIRIS

Ever since I was a child, my grandmother has talked about the Egyptians. She isn't necessarily into the traditional Egyptian myths; rather, she holds that the Egyptians were associated with higher beings that inhabited the earth long ago. Perhaps aliens, perhaps gods, perhaps both. My grandmother believes she has these ideas because she was once one of them. Who knows? She could be right.

One of the gods that my grandmother would have worshiped in the good old days would have been Osiris. He was responsible for civilizing Egypt. It was said that Egypt was cannibalistic until the day he strolled into town and began to teach the people the science of agriculture. He taught them how to cultivate wheat and grapes, but he also taught them how to make tools, how to make bread and, more importantly, how to make wine. The people caught on fast and Osiris was on a roll, so he created a legal system. Since he was a god, he thought it might be advantageous for Egypt to have a system of worship. It was good to be a god.

With Egypt in order, Osiris decided to do the same for the rest of the world, and he set off on his mission. While away, he put his sister, Isis (who was also his wife—gods in those days were limited to a meager population), in charge. Isis ruled well, and when Osiris returned, he was pleased to see all was well in Egypt . . . or was it?

Osiris also had a brother, Seth, who was one bad apple. Seth was extremely jealous of his brother's power and success. Upon the great god's return, unbeknownst to Osiris, Seth took measurements of his brother's physique. Shortly after, a great banquet was held, where Seth revealed a beautiful coffer and said whoever fit into it would own it.

Osiris was first up to try and, of course, slipped in perfectly. No sooner did he do this than Seth and his conspirators nailed down the lid and sealed it in molten lead. The casket was hurried to the river where it floated and eventually reached the ocean. Osiris sailed the seas in his mobile coffin while Isis mourned the loss of her beloved.

Eventually, the coffin came to shore in Phoenicia and nestled up against a tamarisk tree. The tree sensed that this large box was something significant and wrapped its roots around it for protection. Over time, Osiris's tomb became entirely enclosed inside the intuitive tree's trunk.

There Osiris remained, until one day Malcandre, the king of Byblos, saw the enormous trunk and decided that it was exactly what he needed to support his roof. He ordered the tree cut and turned into a pillar. Once installed in his palace, a beautiful aroma emanated from this structure. It was such an amazing smell that it became the talk of the region. Little did the king, or anyone else, know that deep inside the pillar, it was Osiris creating the strange aroma. (Perhaps it was his form of S.O.S.—if so, it worked.)

Isis (literally) got wind of Malcandre's pillar and knew where her brother was. The king was bummed that Isis wanted his famed pillar, but it is not a wise practice for mere mortals to defy the gods.

Once in Egypt, Isis hid the pillar in the swamps of the Nile delta. She opened the trunk, then the casket; inside was her darling Osiris, now dead. Using what powers she had, she attempted to breathe life into him. He came back long enough for the two of them to make love . . . then, he passed.

Shortly thereafter, Seth was wandering through the swamps on a hunting expedition, when he came across the cask of Osiris. He was so enraged that he cut his brother's body into fourteen pieces and scattered them throughout all of Egypt. Horrified, Isis traveled all of Egypt, looking for her de-parted husband (I know, bad joke). Eventually, she found everything but his genitals, which were lost forever. She then managed to resurrect his body, once again.

Osiris approached the gods and appealed to them for justice. Seth was then debunked and Osiris was given the option of returning to earth to rule, but instead chose to become Lord of the Dead, judge of deceased souls. To prepare for his journey to his new realm, Osiris was mummified. Isis did the honors of the embalming and the involved ritual. This was considered to be the first time such a ceremony was ever performed. The dilemma was knowing what to pack . . .

Osiris is considered the Tree of Life, the Axis Munde. The tamarisk tree, and eventually the pillar that housed his body, is a symbol for the connection between heaven and earth. In Christianity, Christ is considered the Axis Munde; in Buddhism, it is Buddha. Most religions offer a symbol or persona that has its foot on both sides of the fence—in tune with the physical as well as the mystical.

I bring this up because artists are always attempting to find this connection. They strive to utilize this tree. They are part of the world but are seeking inspiration from another realm. I see my role as an artist as someone who reaches inside oneself. What I seek is something that is so far inside that it is somewhat foreign—something that is unique and, perhaps, divine. This is when I attempt to climb the Axis Munde.

There is a great Wim Wenders (he's German so it's pronounced "Vim Venders") film called *Wings of Desire* (*City of Angels* was a remake and not nearly as good). The gist of the story is that angels are hovering over Berlin, listening invisibly to the inner testimonies of humans. One angel wants to know what is like to be flesh. He wants to know what it is to feel pleasure and the joy of life, but he also wants to experience, as Hamlet put it, "the heartache and the thousand natural shocks that flesh is heir to."

This is an interesting concept because the idea of the Axis Munde might not just be about climbing to find divine inspiration, but divinity experiencing humanity. Van Gogh might have been inspired by otherworldly sources, but if so, it was only through him that those otherworldly sources could experience the beauty of his paintings. Most (if not all) artists I know believe or want to believe that their creations have more significance than that of a decoration on a wall. They want their work to live beyond them and have the ability to do the truly amazing task of touching the soul of someone else. Have you ever been to a museum and seen a work of art that moved you to tears? Or read a book that changed your perception of life? Or seen a film that inspired you to do something that was truly remarkable? If you have, then you have come across something of great importance; you have come across a Tree of Life.

STRANGE FRUIT

I'm feeling a bit introspective with a subtle dose of melancholy today. Perhaps it is the rain. My mind traces backward into my life a bit as I do some rummaging in the studio. I find an old, old painting I had done in art school. It's pretty bad, but it gets me thinking.

Life is a strange river. I know where I've been but don't know where I'm going. I feel somewhat like Osiris, floating along the river of time. I can see the little twists and turns that have brought me to the place I am now, not only on an emotional or professional level, but on an artistic level. I started as a painter, very expressive, very different from how I am today, though traces remain. It's exciting and yet

a bit sad; the artist that I was is gone. Never again will I see the world in the same way as I did back then . . . for better or for worse. When I look into the past, I often view my past selves in the same way one might view good friends that you no longer keep in touch with—important, but important *then*, not now. How strange it is that I have lost touch with that person who used to paint on canvases. These days, I hang out only with my three-dimensional self . . . he has more depth.

A box is the beginning. I'm not sure what sort of three-dimensional goodies I'll place inside yet. I begin in a slightly unorthodox way, at least for me. I glue some beads around the box

DEPARTMENT STORE

MONKEY TREE— *Okay, have you ever been to a Hobby Lobby or a TJ Maxx? If so, you may have had the same strange experience as I did. I was wandering around the knick-knack sections, looking at all the bizarre stuff, wondering, "Who buys this stuff . . . other than me?" Resin Buddha heads, cast-iron wall decorations, and ornate treasure chests surrounded me. I have to admit, I sometimes feel a bit self-conscious about my purchases (however, not nearly as self-conscious as the time I was doing my series of women's shoe shrines and found myself purchasing twenty pairs of high heel shoes). Now that I think about it, what was even more embarrassing was the time I was creating wearable bra art—bra-ssemblages . . . but I digress. Typically, when you bring a number of strange items up to the register, you get a strange look; the clerk will look you over and sometimes even ask you what in the world you're doing with seventeen tike dolls. I find answering that you're an artist*

and then almost immediately jump right into painting. I think that the nostalgia of my days as a painter has made me want to jump right in there and move some acrylic around. In no time, the box is red with some squiggly designs.

I still feel like painting, so I take a piece of wood and cut it down so that it will fit inside my little red box. Then I begin to paint on it. I add a greenish tint, then I paint some snake design running across the board, a black one with gold stripes. Next, I glue a ruler from a dismantled typewriter beneath the snake. The third dimension is starting to creep in. Bright red rays are added in the center; they emanate from . . . nothing. I am planning on hovering some object, yet to be determined, in front of them.

I hear a scratch at my studio door. My dogs, Lucy and Bart, are soaking wet. They didn't want to come in from the rain half an hour ago, but preferred to lie around in mud, getting drenched. Now that they have that lovely wet-dog smell, they want in. I'm actually surprised they bothered to scratch; Lucy has learned to open the studio door. Bart just follows. Unfortunately, Lucy has not learned to close the door.

The two mutts join me as I work. I've had to block off a portion of my studio to them, so that they don't cut their feet on any sharp objects that might be lying about.

In a large metal file cabinet, I have replaced files with found objects. The doodads in here are special doodads. Not to be used on just any old thing, and certainly not to be given away or thrown out. In here are watch parts, ornate doorknobs and other rarities. Many of the cabinet's contents are items that hold some sentimentality, so for me to use

84

shuts them up right away. They will give you a look, like, "Oh, that explains everything."

On this particular day, I came across some strange palm tree candleholders. The trees sat on a weird little stand that had resin monkeys on all four sides. It looked like an obelisk for some strange group of monkey worshipers. I put about ten of them into my cart and wheeled to the checkout line. "What are you going to do with all these candleholders?" the clerk asked. I replied, "I'm having a dinner party and I need something to serve the bananas in." "Oh," she said and then laughed, realizing it was a joke. After I left, I got to thinking. How cool would it be to actually do that? What a great image: an elegant table complete with palm tree/monkey bananaholders—the bananas partially peeled. One of these days, perhaps, if I find more of them, I'll resist using them in art.

JUNK

them requires that I be really, really certain that the artwork is worthy. Among the items is the belt buckle of my old, now deceased cowboy friend, Judd. Today is its lucky day.

Ever since I started visiting Mexico, I have become fascinated with the heart form. Not cutesy Valentine ones, but ones that are anatomically correct. You see hearts like this on Mexican loteria cards—El Corazon. In Mexico, it doesn't have quite the same meaning. I've always interpreted it to be more like passion that burns from the soul due to divine influence. As it turns out, the heart is also a symbol often used in ancient artworks that depict Osiris. In these works, he is weighing the hearts of the dead. To the Egyptians, the heart was the source of both wisdom and intellect, and therefore it was the best indicator of the true nature of an individual. Because of all this, I insert a photocopy of a large heart in the center of the piece and then paint it red. This will make for a nice cross-cultural reference point (as if any of my work doesn't have this stuff . . .).

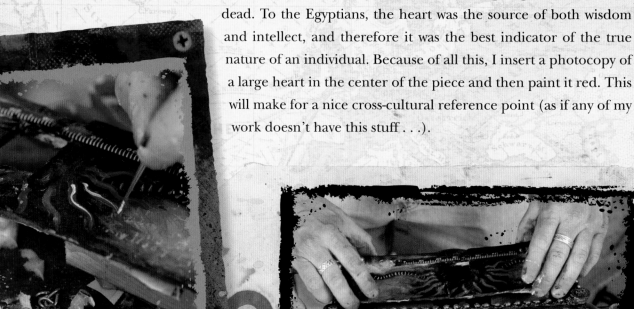

I have to throw an eye in the center of the heart for my own personal visual bias. It's appropriate, nonetheless. After I glue down the eye, I attach a brass washer on top of it to frame it.

I can't count the number of times someone has seen a tiny hand in my work and wondered where I got it. Typically, they look like they are gold or rock or wood or rusty metal. The funny thing is that these hands, in every single instance, are 25-cent doll hands, which can be found at any craft store. One advantage of me being a painter before I became a sculptor is that I learned a long time ago that paint can make anything look like anything. A couple of hands, one on either end of the ruler, will do nicely, and, of course, I paint them. Black first, then a drybrush of gold on top.

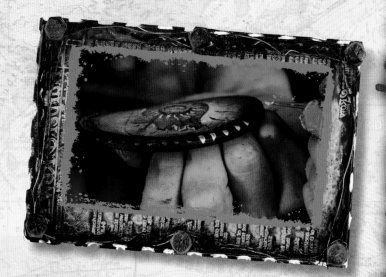

JUDD

BELT BUCKLE— How I acquired the belt buckle is really not a very interesting story. It was broken and given to me by a friend, who knew I could use it in a piece of art. What is interesting is the person who gave it to me.

Once in a while, you come across someone who has had a really fascinating life. In my bartending years, I met a number of people who fit this bill. One such guy was a man named Judd. He was ninety-some when I met him and lived to the ripe old age of 10-1, though his wife, Grace, had to remind him of his age periodically. Born in the back of a wagon during a Montana blizzard, he had a story for everything—stories of moving to California in the 1920s and working as a lifeguard at Venice Beach, stories of living in California as a young teen, even a story of auditioning for "The Little Rascals."

Most of his stories were about his ranching days in Montana. He called himself a "cowpuncher." This is apparently the same as a cowpoke, but cowpuncher is the preferred term. He related

The box looks okay, but not great. One of the most dramatic changes that occurred when I abandoned my days as a canvas painter was that I started thinking outside of the box—literally. I started needing to extend the artwork beyond the limits of a frame. This piece requires such a treatment.

I think that it is time to use one of the monkey trees. Those monkey tree candleholders have been staring me down for months. Time to put them to use. I decide the *Wizard of Oz* monkey is not what I need, just the palm tree. I take my Dremel and begin to slice the palm tree from the base. Yikes, nothing like cutting through cast resin. The dust is too much. Time to take this out into the rain. Fortunately, I had recently purchased a cordless Dremel. Next thing I know, I am being covered in rain and white dust. Better on my clothes than in my lungs.

The tree is painted in the same manner as the hands. Then it is placed, glued and screwed to the top of the box. I grab the Dremel again and slice off a few resin fronds from the candleholder. These are placed on the side of the piece. A little metal fixture is attached below and painted with root imagery, just for fun.

The work is more or less complete. I'm not sure that I really like this particular process. I don't think that I like working backwards (I suppose it could be for-wards for some people). Don't get me wrong, I really like the result, I'm just unsure I like how I got to the result. I more or less knew the color scheme before I added the objects. It was all very well planned. In some ways, the process was a lot easier than normal. Maybe this is the downside. When I have to battle the work it can often lead to surprises and experimentations that don't come from a process of pre-planning. As much as I complain about the tug-o-war between the art and me, I think I really need it in order to feel like I accomplished something worthwhile. In this case, I think I have something worthwhile, but it came without a crescendo.

horrible tales of sub-zero storms that would freeze standing cows to the ground where they stood, and he wasn't able to help them.

For those interested in Montana history, Judd and Grace had an unlimited supply of tales. They had a bit of Mexican history to share, since they spent quite a bit of time south of the border as well. I remember one funny account of Judd walking into a cantina that smelled of urine. He complained to the bartender/owner about the smell. The owner shrugged his shoulders and said, "Señor, who eats the smell?"

I'm not sure how much fabrication went on in old Judd's stories, and I can't tell you how many times I heard the same accounts over and over again. But I didn't mind; he was a pure joy to serve highballs to.

To Ben

SKELETON WOMAN

This is an Inuit tale that begins with a tragic act of violence. A man struggled to drag his daughter to the edge of a cliff and threw her into the sea. The young woman screamed as she plummeted into the water; then, with a splash . . . silence, as she sank into a strange underwater realm. The ocean is not kind to the flesh of humans. Sea creatures fed on her skin, fish plucked out her eyes; eventually, she was nothing but a skeleton cradled in a bed of barnacles. For one hundred years, she rocked back and forth on the ocean floor. Her bones were covered in crustaceans, and strange sea creatures lived in the sockets that once housed her eyes. The girl's beautiful, long, black hair had long disappeared, and in its place grew strands of seaweed, flowing with the ocean tide.

Fishermen steered their boats away from this haunted inlet, in response to the tales of the grotesque skeleton woman who wandered the waters, and who surely brought men to their doom. But one day, a young fisherman drifted into the haunted bay. He was hungry—so hungry, he figured that there would be excellent fishing in an area that no one chose to troll.

The young man's lone boat drifted through the cold water of the deserted bay. He felt a strange chill down his spine, when suddenly his hook snagged something. Something big. He started to pull up what he thought to be the catch of a lifetime. He pulled and pulled. Far below, his hook had snagged a rib of the skeleton woman. She resisted, but the more she fought, the more tangled her body became.

The fisherman kept pulling. He looked into the water to catch a glimpse of his prize fish, but all he could see was a bit of seaweed and the glow of something white. Finally, after a mighty pull, the tangled skeleton woman latched on to the side of the boat. Shocked and frightened, the man grabbed an oar and pushed the boney woman back into the sea. The fisherman started rowing like a maniac to get back to shore, not realizing that just below the water's surface, the skeleton woman was trailing behind him. The faster he rowed, the faster the bones followed.

Exhausted upon reaching the shore, the fisherman grabbed his pole and started to run over the icy terrain. A strange rattling sound seemed to follow him. He turned to look behind him, and to his dread, he saw the skeleton woman, her bones clicking and clacking as she scurried after him. The fisherman was so filled with terror, he didn't realize she was still tangled in his fishing line. He needed only to drop his pole and her pursuit would desist.

At last, he reached his home and rushed inside. He remained still, listening for the dreadful rattling . . . nothing. Only the sound of his heart pounding, which he feared would give him away. Finally feeling at ease, he lit a fire. Once lit, he was startled by the sight of a jumbled pile of bones heaped in the corner. His fear was oddly replaced by a tremendous feeling of compassion for this poor creature. He untangled the skeleton woman's bones from the fishing line and respectfully laid her body out and covered her in warm furs. Exhausted from the day's events, the fisherman fell fast asleep.

Through the night, the fire warmed the skeleton woman's bones; it had seemed an eternity since she had last felt the warmth of a fire. She watched as the man slept. His eyes began to move under his lids. He was dreaming. She hoped it was a good dream, even though he had bonked her on the head with a paddle . . . Ultimately, she had to admit, he had treated her quite kindly.

She started to drift off to sleep, when she noticed a low drumming sound. Bah-bum, bah-bum. It was the fisherman's heart. She was enchanted by the sound. Bah-bum, bah-bum. Slowly, she crawled across the floor toward the dreaming man's side. When she was next to him, she reached into his chest and took out his heart. With great care, she tapped on the heart and sang, "Flesh, flesh, flesh." As she sang, flesh grew back onto her bones; her seaweed mane was replaced by the beautiful black hair she once had; her lovely dark brown eyes returned to her sockets. She had returned to the woman that she was before her father threw her into the sea.

The woman then crawled beneath the furs that covered the man and embraced him. In the morning, the two awoke and from that moment forward, their souls were joined; they would never part.

Full fathom five thy father lies;

Of his bones are coral made;

Those are pearls that were his eyes:

Nothing of him that doth fade

But doth suffer a sea-change

Into something rich and strange.

This is from Shakespeare's *The Tempest*. It is my favorite quotation of all time. Why? Well, for one, it is a great metaphor for mortality; secondly, it is a great metaphor for the process of assemblage. In both cases, it's about transformation—a shift of realities. What once was must perish, but fear not, a new strange existence awaits; nothing is completely annihilated.

The skeleton woman transforms from a girl to a strange creature of the sea, and then is transformed into the soulmate of the fisherman. This is the transformation that takes place in a piece of assemblage. It all begins with an object that has a definitive function; eventually, that existence passes—by choice, by force or by time. The young woman is discarded like an old toaster, and eventually the old existence is lost. The woman, like the object, decays, for days, years or centuries. Then, along comes an artist like me who finds this item, and eventually it's given a new, more significant existence.

But wait. Was it the fisherman, acting as artist, who transformed the discarded entity? Or was it the skeleton woman, a discarded entity, who transformed the fisherman/artist? Perhaps it was a bit of both. It is true that a found object must be nurtured for it to become a piece of art, but it is also true that the object must speak. It must reach into the heart, touch the artist and speak to him in order for meaningful transformation to take place.

The term *sculpt* technically means "to take away"; it is really a subtractive process. The idea is that an artist like Michelangelo carves through the marble to find the hidden artwork inside. Assemblage, on the other hand, is an additive art form; items are combined to create a final piece of work. Even so, I see my goal as similar to that of a sculptor. As strange as it may seem, to me, each object has a soul to it, and it is my job to find it and bring it back to life in a new way. No longer forgotten, no longer without purpose.

STRANGE ATTRACTIONS

A winter-y feel—that is what originally came to mind when I thought of the art to go with this myth. The tale takes place in an icy, arctic setting. Even the idea of a skeleton at the bottom of the sea sends shivers. Then, metaphorically, what could possibly be colder than death itself? Because of the very nature of the tale, my gut told me to approach this tale in tones of white-blues and grays, the colors that would give the feel of ice and snow.

STUDIO TRASH CAN

LIQUID NAILS TUBES— *Everyone who knows me is aware of my love affair with Liquid Nails. These days there are a bajillion different adhesives created by this company, but the one I really love is the good, old-fashioned, original formula. It's a nice adhesive, but it's also great for creating an interesting, chunky texture. I usually buy this stuff in the caulk gun tubes because I go through so much of it. The result is a studio filled with empty adhesive canisters.*

My mission typically is to try and see past an object's function and take in what it's made of— what kind of shapes it has. (In other words, not see a teakettle, but see the forms that make up the teakettle.) This is an important practice when I'm scavenging, but sometimes something is so familiar that it is difficult to see past the function. This was true with the empty adhesive tubes. These were trash; when the glue was gone, they served no purpose.

One day, however, staring at a trash can full of discarded canisters, something changed. I realized it was such an incredible

I'm about ninety percent positive this is the direction I will take, but first I have to figure out what objects I want to use. I don't even have a clue about the shape. Let's start with a basic box.

I find a box that once housed a bottle of Booker's bourbon. Smooth, strong and buttery. This booze was a staple at my home during the first weekend of May. Why? The Kentucky Derby, of course. I used to have an annual party, complete with fancy hats, seersucker suits, gambling and mint juleps. It was a fun time. One of the annual attendees was Steve Glueckert, a Missoula artist who could best be described as a found-object toymaker for adults. His work has a playful quality that is enhanced by his use of gears, levers and cranks to make his artwork come alive with motion. He would always show up with

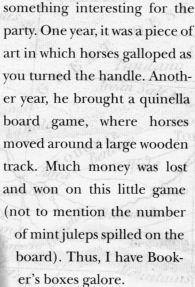

something interesting for the party. One year, it was a piece of art in which horses galloped as you turned the handle. Another year, he brought a quinella board game, where horses moved around a large wooden track. Much money was lost and won on this little game (not to mention the number of mint juleps spilled on the board). Thus, I have Booker's boxes galore.

I start crashing about, piling through junk. I find one of those Tin Man hat funnels, and it fits perfectly over the box. Sold.

I have been using foam insulation like crazy as of late, so why not stick with a good thing? Later, after the foam has set, I sit back and look at the work. This is as important as moving paint around or adhering objects. Sometimes an artist just needs to sit back and ponder. It's like trying to speak to it. Kind of like the Disneyland Haunted Mansion ride where the medium says, "Rap on a table, it's time to respond, send us a message, from regions beyond!" As I do this, the shape of this newly formed object is reminding me of something . . . It is so familiar. What could it be? Well, I grab my caulk gun of Liquid Nails and begin to work. Suddenly, it dawns on me. It looks like a giant Liquid Nails caulk tube. This gives me a great idea. I have trash cans filled with

empty canisters. Why not frame the box in with a tube on each side? *Bueno!*

I decide that I am going to light the interior of the box and place a skeleton form inside. The light will be below the figure, creating a campfire look. The front of the box is treated in such a way that it seems like the viewer is looking into a cave; inside, skeleton woman sits. For now, I'll mount the

waste, and that something could be done with these forms. I was suddenly living in the present. No longer was the empty Liquid Nails tube a container that once held adhesive, waiting to reach the landfill. Now, it just was. Suddenly, I could see it, really see it. It became beautiful. Suddenly, I became totally absorbed in its object-ness; its future was no longer bleak.

How many other things had I overlooked? Moments like this are little awakenings; they are tiny Zen moments. What was it that clicked and allowed me to "see" on that day? I must have had a little extra dose of Eastern philosophy that particular morning. Come to think of it, it was probably when I was on a green tea binge. (You remember the time when you couldn't turn on a morning show without seeing a segment about the stuff?) Now I'm back to coffee. I wonder if I would still see objects in the same Zen manner? Who cares—it's time for my quadruple macchiato.

95

skeleton on a separate piece of wood to be added later. This way, I'll be able to paint and adorn without having to cram my hand through the little cave opening.

In the interim, I have come to the conclusion that winter colors are not going to do the trick. I really want to emphasize the heat of the fire, and the love that burns between the skeleton woman and the fisherman. I go for a yellow-gold wash over the whole thing. How it will evolve from this color remains to be seen.

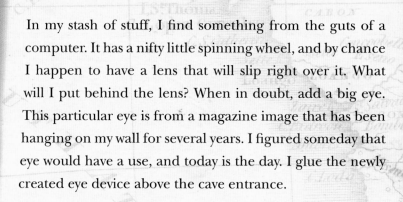

In my stash of stuff, I find something from the guts of a computer. It has a nifty little spinning wheel, and by chance I happen to have a lens that will slip right over it. What will I put behind the lens? When in doubt, add a big eye. This particular eye is from a magazine image that has been hanging on my wall for several years. I figured someday that eye would have a use, and today is the day. I glue the newly created eye device above the cave entrance.

The interior is next. I find a man's image and I glue it to the wood. It sits above and behind the skeleton woman. Scraps of paper are added. Then I take some white paint and begin adding some radiating images coming from the man. Numbers are glued on either side of the fisherman. I am using numbers because something about them reminds me of the lottery . . . thus, fate and the wheel of fortune.

BRAD'S CAR

TAP HANDLE— *Living in the Northwest, especially in a college town, the microbrewery trend hit my fair city of Missoula like gangbusters (a phrase I've never used in a written format before— just thought you'd like to know).*

While I was in college, one brewery I was particularly fond of was based out of Oregon—Rogue Ales. I first came across it in Ashland, Oregon, when I was attending the Shakespeare Festival. I loved their beer, and I found that whoever was in charge of their marketing had a great sense of humor. The day of this initial visit, I was swilling a pint of Shakespeare Stout—delicious. From that point on, I was hooked. Whenever a new beer came out, I was there.

It's an established fact that I have a Day of the Dead fetish. Perhaps it is because I spend so much time in Mexico for Dia de los Muertos, or perhaps I spend so much time in Mexico because I have this fetish. I love all the skeletal toys, and how death is feared and mocked in the same breath. Love it.

I am struggling with finding a way to somehow visually connect the woman to the man. I find an arm image from a CD cover that I don't hesitate to cut up. It is a reddish arm holding a heart. It doesn't dawn on me till later that the hand holding the heart is the most appropriate thing I could have used for the myth; she takes out the fisherman's heart and plays it like a drum. First off, the fact that I had something with that exact image on it is pretty amazing. Secondly, the fact that I subliminally used it without any conscious connection gives me the sensation that a sleepwalker might have: "I did what?" I wonder if I was in some trance.

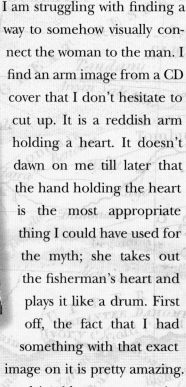

I place a book of matches at the base of her feet. At this point, they have not been lit; this changes in a literal flash. I use the heat gun to dry some paint, and whoosh. They ignite. No worries. No damage. In fact, it made a few areas look better. A happy accident.

I have a very difficult task before me. I need eyes to cover the skeleton's hollow eyes. As it is, it is too scary. Now it's back to the search for the perfect eyes. Finally, I find some that I think will work and glue them on.

As I do this, a phone call comes in from a friend who tells me that a typewriter has been spotted in such and such an alley. With no further ado, I hop into the car to save the abandoned

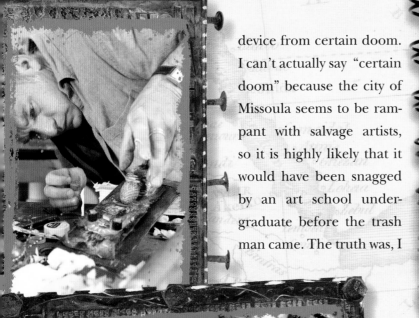

device from certain doom. I can't actually say "certain doom" because the city of Missoula seems to be rampant with salvage artists, so it is highly likely that it would have been snagged by an art school undergraduate before the trash man came. The truth was, I just had to beat out the other artists.

Back to the eyes. The ones I glued on are too serious. I sigh heavily, for I know what is ahead of me: hours of more eye hunting. It's such a challenge because I want to create the perfect expression. (Oh, and also,

Well, you could imagine my elation when I discovered that Rogue had created a brew honoring the Day of the Dead, called Dead Guy Ale. The bottle used the image of a Mayan skeleton with a beehive headdress, atop a wooden beer keg—very enticing for someone with my likes. And guess what? Delicious to boot! (My mouth is watering just thinking about the beer—I might need to go pick up a bottle later today.) Eventually Rogue came out with some very cool tap handles for this product using the same image, but cast in plastic. Well, once I saw these boney little dudes, I had one thing on my mind—how on earth can I get my hands on one of those tap handles?

One interesting tradition among male college students is the use of tap handles as automobile stick shifts. I had a friend, Brad, who was the king of this ritual. He started out using the basic domestic taps then worked his way into the exports, and when the micros started popping up, he was in heaven. He had a job in a bar, so he had easy access to any handle he wanted.

I have the challenge of somehow making a *skull* feel caring and compassionate.) In general, I have to make a skeleton woman seem beautiful.

I ponder this while I change the cave color to a rust tone. From there, I turn my attention to the electrical cord that runs out of the bottom of the piece. There was a time when I would have left it as is. Now, however, thanks to the advice of a curator friend, I have changed my tune. Her point was that a cord is visually part of the piece, so when

the artwork is displayed, the cord needs to either be hidden or it should somehow feel like it is part of the work. I took this to heart, and the solution that I have come up with is wrapping the cord with a heavy gauge metal wire. For my work, it is ideal. It actually looks as if a piece of barbed wire is coming out of the artwork. Even better is that it can be shaped, so the cord can cascade down the wall in whatever design you bend into it.

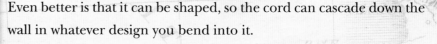

Three months later, seven thousand sets of eyes later, I think I found it. A set of old encyclopedias contained the perfect eyes. When I saw them, I would have never guessed they would be the right pair, but once I placed them over the skull, everything I wanted occurred. The skeleton is actually somewhat attractive; well, as much as a skeleton can be attractive.

One day, he stopped by to pick me up. I got into his car and, behold, it was the Holy Grail of tap handles: the Dead Guy Ale skeleton. Thou shalt not covet thy buddy's tap handle. I was coveting, baby.

The Rogue tap was beautiful but a little awkward. It sat a little bit high and was somewhat bulky for a functional stick shift. Watching him yank that skeleton around was a bit unnerving. Well, sure enough, he broke it. All it took was a sharp shift to third and "snap," the head popped off. My hand searched under my seat. There it was, poor little guy, but it was a clean break. Immediately, I chimed in and said I could find a way to fix it. I was an artist, after all.

Brad agreed, and put it into my capable hands. Sucker. A little glue and it was in my Dia de los Muertos collection in no time. Hey, it wasn't like Brad was that good of a friend.

To Bernie

102

VISHNU DREAMING

In Hinduism, it is told that in a cosmic sea, a rather large serpent floats. This is Shesha, the snake, whose cobra-like hood is actually composed of hundreds of heads. Inside that massive hood, all the planets of the universe exist. Underneath this massive hood reclines the deity Vishnu.

Vishnu is one-third of a very important Hindu trinity, a trinity that essentially allows all things to exist . . . and not exist. First, there is the god Brahma; he has one head but four faces (in case you're wondering about the arrangement: one on the front, one on the back and one on each side). Brahma is the creator god. It is he that initiates all things into existence.

Next comes the great blue god (the color of the sky), Vishnu, the preserver. It is his role to maintain the universe. He is, for all intents and purposes, everything. All of existence is he, and he is everything and everywhere. When the world goes out of whack, he jumps in as an Avatar (a living incarnation) and tries to mend the ailments of the world.

Finally, there is Shiva, the destroyer. He puts an end to all things. Sure it sounds bad, but it is also viewed as a purifying force. Through his destruction, he ends the evil in the universe and allows for Brahma to create anew.

Combined, they form a trinity that is the single perpetual cycle from creation to destruction and back to creation again. They are past, present and future all in one.

The story goes that Vishnu reclines on the very comfortable Shesha. Some say that he is sleeping, but actually he is performing a very vital function. He is dreaming. What is of interest is the subject of his dream. He is dreaming the universe. He is not dreaming about the universe; he is actually dreaming the universe into existence. All thing that are exist in Vishnu's dream. As he envisions all things, suddenly a beautiful lotus begins to grow from his navel. It grows, and a large flower begins to bud. When the petals open, sitting inside is the creator god, Brahma.

Brahma's role is to bring Vishnu's dream into reality. Creation is a seemingly simple process to Brahma; it is a mere blink of his eyes and all that Vishnu imagined becomes manifest. At the beginning of each day, Brahma opens his eyes and a world is created. At the end of each day, he closes his eyes and a world is destroyed.

Here's where the story gets interesting for those into math. It is said that a day for Brahma lasts 4,320,000,000 years; this is said to be the lifespan of the universe. Universe after universe is created as Brahma opens his eyes in the morning and closes them in the evening, and he does this for one hundred years—one hundred of his years. This adds up to 311 trillion years. We are on year 51 (155 trillion) since he started his cycle of creation. I'm not sure how far along we are on this particular Brahma day (the age of the current universe), but I am sure someone has figured that out.

Back to the lotus: after one hundred Brahma years, his life will end, and the lotus will close and return to Vishnu's navel. The end of all things. This is where Shiva steps in, but not for long. After a time, Vishnu will dream again, a new lotus will grow and Brahma will once again start creating worlds for another 311 trillion years. New worlds will arise again and again. Seems like an eternity.

The story of Vishnu dreaming the universe is somewhat of a mind trip. The concept that the universe and all that it holds are the conceptions of Vishnu is pretty heavy stuff. Then again, much of Hinduism is; the universe, according to Hindu myths and beliefs, is no simple structure. What an amazing idea to imagine that all that I know, and all that I will know, stems from the thoughts of a deity reclining on a cosmic serpent.

Consider inspiration. I think of an idea, and wonder about its source. Does it come from divinity? Does it come to me because Vishnu dreamt of me dreaming of that bright idea? And what of Vishnu? Is he the source of all inspiring thoughts, or did some other entity dream of Vishnu? It's like looking into a mirror with a mirror behind you—a never-ending tunnel.

Then of course there is the thought of all those things in my dreams. Does a lotus grow from my navel, as well? Are worlds created from my dreams? Well, yes. I too bring ideas into fruition. As an artist, thoughts are often made manifest.

I see my role as bringing ideas into the light for others to experience. I must be part Vishnu and part Brahma. (Don't think poor Shiva is left out in the cold.)

Destruction is essential to the creative process as well. On the obvious level of being an artist who uses deconstructed items, this is apparent, but it is also true on a deeper level. As an artist, my role is to challenge the status quo. I am constantly questioning the norm; it is the need to break from the past to create anew. One works and works and works. Eventually it is time to question one's artwork and explore a different direction. The art world would be quite different if Picasso merely continued working in a very realistic fashion, as opposed to exploring Cubism. And what of Van Gogh, if he didn't explore the heavy use of color and paint? In both cases, these artists destroyed what they knew so that creation was fresh. It is the risk that made all the difference in the world. You know the line about the road less traveled. This is Shiva.

To be an artist, one must be Brahma, Vishnu, Shiva, Brahma, Vishnu, Shiva, Brahma, Vishnu, Shiva . . . Whew, I need a nap. Know any good snakes?

THE IMPORTANCE OF ZZZS

I've been thinking (a thought bubble now appears over my head), and to really emphasize the concept of Vishnu dreaming the universe, I need to incorporate a thought bubble over his head. When I picked up that scale in Ginger's Antique Store, that's what popped into my head: a thought bubble. After all, it has a nice little window to view into. Ideally, it would be great to have the image change and move. But I'm not going to mess with that.

GINGER'S

BATHROOM SCALE— *Along Highway 200 in the Sun River Valley, not far from Great Falls, Montana, there used to be a place called Ginger's Antique Store. Whenever I was driving through, I would pull off the road and do a little junkin'.*

What a great place. The building was built sometime in the 1800s (I'm told 1890) and was painted bright red. Whenever I drove past it, I was reminded of that scene in the Clint Eastwood film "High Plains Drifter" where the entire town is painted red, and a sign with the town name Lago is replaced with the word "Hell." I have to admit that before I had ever stopped, it kind of gave me the creeps because of that scene.

Finally, one day I did stop in. It was a Sunday morning around eleven. I was amazed at the size of the antique/secondhand portion of the shop. It was enormous and filled with

Moving parts can be trouble. If someone has purchased a piece from you with moving parts, you have to worry about the possibility of replacement or repair. It's much easier to repair a scratch or re-glue a doodad; in fact, you can walk people through the process over the phone. But try doing that with a mechanism. Don't think so.

I want only the faceplate of the scale, so I dissect it. Always an enjoyable part of the process—destruction. I'm not one of those screw-by-screw dissectors, either. Give me the sledge or Dremel, and let's rip the thing apart. Such fun.

It would be nice to mount the scale onto something. It needs a square to contain the oval shape. Hey, that gives me an

idea. I'll use the oval shape to visually represent the hood of the serpent Shesha, and then I can frame it in with the box shape. Might as well use that drum case or tambourine case or whatever musical instrument it was for.

So I'm thinking a round crown or fan-like shape that comes off of the case and reiterates the oval scale's shape. The piece that I think would work well is that inexpensive serving tray I picked up a TJ Maxx; I'll slice it in half and plop it on top.

Time to get grooving with screws and Liquid Nails. Now that gives me a great idea for a new product. Liquid *Screws*, which would be the ultimate adhesive. Don't ask me how it would work, but it would be cool . . . I digress. The whirl of the power drill, and I sink some screws through the beginning objects into the case. Now a whole helluva lot of Liquid Nails.

Next, some ornamentation. I want the box to feel like some weird device from the late 1800s and early 1900s. Inventions of that era fascinate me. Half the time, it was impossible to tell what the device was, but it looked beautiful and it seemed as if the decoration of the device took more time to create than the actual gadget. Back to the whole idea of mechanisms. Perhaps what I need to do is hook up with

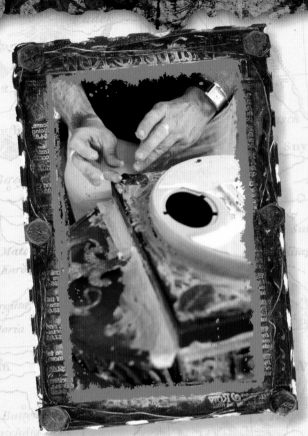

amazing things. I still regret not purchasing a huge section of post office boxes, complete with beautiful ornate doors and locks. It would have been a steal at 150 smackers, but I was broke at the time.

What I didn't mention was that I was extremely hungover that day, and was wandering around somewhat zombie-like at that time. Now, the only thing that really cures me of a severe hangover is a Bloody Mary. I crave them when I'm in that state. So there I was, pretending to be interested in old compasses, when suddenly I saw the Holy Grail of Bloody Marys. A shopper was walking around with a beautiful, reddish-brown elixir, complete with olives, peppers and a honkin' stalk of celery. (I must say it has been a disappointment in recent years, because many bars have stopped using the celery stalk. Shame on them. It is the stalk that makes the Mary.) I looked at the guy and wondered where one was to acquire such a libation. Then I realized, of course, attached to the

an inventor and just create the housings for his/her creations. That would be a pretty interesting gig. (As a sidenote, I just love those automated, early 1900s gypsy fortunetellers. I would love to have one for the house.) But, I'm off on a tangent again. I need another cup of joe . . .

Okay, some metal leaves for the corners, and a cast-iron whatchama thingy to go in front of the tray shape. Now I want to splash on some paint. It will help give me a bit of direction. Blue

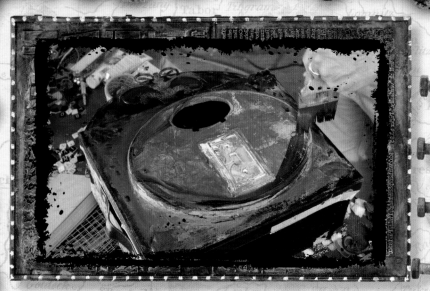

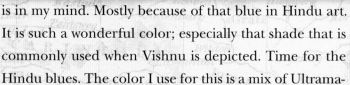

is in my mind. Mostly because of that blue in Hindu art. It is such a wonderful color; especially that shade that is commonly used when Vishnu is depicted. Time for the Hindu blues. The color I use for this is a mix of Ultramarine Blue with some white and a smidge of Dioxazine Purple. I find that it is best to surround this color with areas that have some nice greenish tints to make the Hindu Blue glow. Usually a mixture of Phthalo Green and Ultramarine Blue. First I need to get some lightness onto the objects, so I paint it whitish for a primer (actually, I got a bit of green-blue mixed in so it will be more of a light aqua).

When I was in art school, they talked about the imprimatura, which is the first layer of paint added after a canvas is gessoed. It is a transparent wash of color that sets the overall hue of the piece. In this case, the aqua color is actually working as the light gesso layer, so now I'm going to add an imprimatura layer of bluish green—a nice watery wash of Ultramarine Blue and Pthalo Green.

Wow. That gave it a really nice oceanic feel. Now I am really hankering to see how that Hindu blue goes with it. I think I'll frame in the scale with a pure version of the blue/purple/white, then bring in a more subtle washed version throughout the rest of the piece.

It's interesting the way I paint because I paint like I assemble. Basically, I see paint as another object. I don't do much color mixing

antique store is Ginger's Bar. So
I wandered past the milk glass
section and went into the tavern.

It was a great old space, and the
back bar was riddled with stupid
bar joke signs and girly posters.
Also on the shelves behind the bar
was a huge spice collection of, you
guessed it, ginger—hundreds of
different brands.

I ordered my drink, and I
was ready to shop. I remember
thinking how nice it would be if
I could do all my shopping this
way. Ultimately, I didn't really
buy much. A scale that was a
mere 25 cents, a bunch of little
knick-knacks, and some strange
vintage radio device. But that's

109

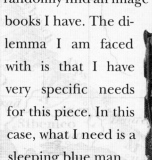

on the "canvas." Rather, I do it in layers. It doesn't really matter if it is a translucent wash or a white or light design pattern. I usually work something like this: I add a wash, then paint a design (the design could include writing), then I add another wash, then another design, then another wash, and so on and so on. Painting this way creates a rich image with a lot of depth. It reminds me of looking through time. Hints of the past are still present, but only subtly. If it is done properly, it can be like looking through sea water, where different elements float at different depths; the images become more and more obscure the deeper one looks.

I am really pleased with the blues. Now I need to think about Vishnu, and I decide to frame him in, though I have no idea what I'm going to use for his image. Off to the computer to look for photos. Not my favorite thing to do. I would much rather randomly find an image in the piles upon piles of magazines and books I have. The dilemma I am faced with is that I have very specific needs for this piece. In this case, what I need is a sleeping blue man.

Two hours later, still on the computer. The problem was

This certifies that the fire equipment was serviceable condition on the date noted.

finding the right closed eyes. I feel like Goldilocks. Too big, too brown, too blah blah blah. Searching. Searching. I pull up twenty different sets of sleeping eyes and print them out. I try them out on the piece, and I don't like any of them. Back to the comput-

er, and pull up another ten sets of eyes. Finally, one set from this batch works. I mount the eyes on a small rectangle of wood and plop them on the now blue portrait.

A few more items get added: a little keyhole thingy (I have no recollection where it spawned from), magazine and dictionary images for the dream bubble, and various other doodads.

One thing that I still need to do is address the Shesha/scale area. I have already added a copper conduit coming out of the base of the case, to create a snaky feel. What really needs to happen is a hooded cobra effect; in particular, a cobra with multiple heads. A box of metal sheaths comes to mind. Not really sure

okay, because the drink was damn good, and my headache magically disappeared. All was right in the world. Especially after the second one.

WILD CHICKENS

PERCUSSION CASE— *The Wild Chickens were, and sometimes still are, a band in Missoula. The name comes from the fact that, at one time, all the members worked as prep cooks in the same restaurant. They spent many an hour chopping up chickens. Of course, man cannot live on poultry parts alone; one must have sustenance for the soul. So began the Wild Chickens. Year after year, they played at local bars and friends' weddings. I've even heard them play acoustic sets—sort of a Wild Chickens: Uncooked, you might say.*

how they were intended to be used, but somehow these little hollow phallic devices are used in planting. I have a number of them, so I lay them across the oval scale in a fan-like design. Then I run some rope from each one and wrap the pieces together so that they converge. Visually, though not physically, they seem to grow from the conduit. Excellent. The whole piece seems plant-like. This addition unifies the whole thing. The lower part grows up like a stem into the cobra forms, which almost seems like a lotus. Appropriate.

This brings up an interesting point, because it is pretty nifty how sometimes things subliminally occur. For instance, the lotus/cobra design was not intended, but it magically happened. Somehow, I merged two crucial elements of the myth into one form. I wonder if it was really my subconscious or if it was actually the very nature of the myth. I wonder if the visual elements inherent in the story intentionally correlate. For instance, is the multi-headed cobra deliberately supposed to relate to the concept of the lotus? It could be. It could be the Jungian Collective Unconscious at work; this is the part of the unconscious, according to Jung, that is common in all humans. It is supposed to house forms and symbols (archetypes) that are occurring in all cultures throughout history. Are the lotus and the cobra symbols that somehow relate to something inherent inside me? Personally I say: Absolutely. The reason I believe it to be true is that my art is derived from non-specific ideas. I don't typically use allegories; rather, I use intuitive and personal symbols. What is bizarre is that people

can look at my work and know what I am trying to say metaphorically. Something definitely appears to be happening on a deeper level. Once again, more evidence that art is just one crazy magical mystery tour.

Time ebbed on until, one by one, the members started to move on. And so it was, the Chickens eventually were no more.

Once in a while, the members get back together and have a Wild Chickens reunion. All the old groupies show up for the event, me included. I mention these guys because one of the guys in the band, Brian, always supplied me with interesting discarded instruments and sound equipment. He would usually roll up in his Subaru station wagon, filled with musical thingies for me to choose from. Through the years, I have acquired an enormous bounty from these hatchback giveaways. It took me a number of years to figure out what to do with the percussion case, but I knew that I would eventually come up with something because I love boxes and suitcases.

113

To my parents

CAN THE FLOWERS SE

ZANAHARY

The primary creator in traditional Madagascan mythology is a chap named Zanahary. I can envision this deity sitting around one afternoon (or whatever it was called before the sun, not to mention time, existed), twiddling his thumbs. So he hunkered down and started creating. He started with the heavens, creating the sun, the sky and the stars. Next came planet Earth. He built towering mountains, vast and deep oceans, flowing rivers, as well as plants, trees and flowers of every variety; he created everything we know in the natural world except for animals and humans. After this long project, Zanahary was quite pleased with himself and returned to heaven to do whatever creators do in heaven.

The earth was fertile, so fertile that it grew a new deity, Ratovoantany. Ratovoantany liked what he saw of his new digs. He walked up and down the coast. He climbed all the mountains. He swam through streams. But something was missing. Ratovoantany grew lonely and bored, and one day he decided it was time to take up a project of his own.

Meanwhile, Zanahary was lounging in the sky, when he heard something. Intrigued, he swooped down to check out what was causing the noise. What Zanahary saw was a bit bewildering. He saw the self-created Ratovoantany covered in mud, making little human and animal figures from clay.

Zanahary was impressed on several levels. He was impressed with the ability of Ratovoantany to create himself, and Zanahary was quite delighted with Ratovoantany's artistry and innovation. He decided to introduce himself. "What are those interesting little things you're making? I really like them."

Ratovoantany blushed. "Well, thank you. I decided I'd make some pals. It can get kind of quiet down here."

Picking up a clay figure, Zanahary said, "You are quite the artist, but I bet you hear that all the time."

Ratovoantany turned a deeper shade of red. "No, actually you're the first."

"What do you call these things?"

"The one you're holding is a lemur, in that pile are humans, over there are pigs and I've just started working on bugs." Ratovoantany lifted up a centipede.

"How would you feel if I took these with me to my place in the heavens? I have the perfect place for them—good lighting, and they wouldn't get broken."

"Well, I'm honored that you like them, but I really can't part with them. It would be like giving up part of myself. No offense, I'm sure you have a nice place and all."

Zanahary thought for a moment. "What would you say if I told you that I could give them life? Hmmm? These little guys would be jumping, hopping, crawling and flying in no time. Pretty cool, huh?"

"Don't get me wrong, that is really a cool idea, but no thanks. Besides, look at the craftsmanship."

"Okay, you drive a tough bargain. How does this sound? We split them. You build them. I'll give them life. You can have them for a time, and then I get them for my collection. Every time you make a new one, I'll give it life, then it goes in my collection. It's going to get pretty crowded down here if you keep making them. What do you say? Hmmm? Do we have a deal?"

Secretly, he had always envisioned them animated; plus, it would sure relieve his loneliness. So that is how humans and animals were created.

There was one thing that Zanahary wasn't totally upfront about, however. Sometimes Zanahary would attempt to take the creations earlier than expected. Of course, this upset Ratovoantany, who wouldn't let this happen without a fight.

So there you have it—the ancient battle between heaven and earth. Ratovoantany attempted to keep his creations on the earth as long as possible and out of Zanahary's reach. Life is so fragile.

115

On a very simple metaphoric level, what we have here is an artist creating something of value, and along comes the Zanahary Corporation, which wants to promote the art form. Ratovoantany gets a big contract to sign, makes a little cabbage, but ultimately Zanahary is the only one who wins the prize. This said, let's not dwell on that cynical, twenty-first-century version of the tale, because there are more interesting things to talk about.

When I first heard the Madagascan myth, an image of a child making mud pies came to mind. I can remember being a young boy in the stereotypical striped shirt and shorts playing in mounds of mud. Entire universes were created out of this base, raw and even gross material. My mother was not so thrilled with me after a day's work, but she didn't understand the seriousness of what I was accomplishing. No adult could. I remember times when the process of play was a meditative, timeless state in which the "real world" ceased to exist. All that existed was my mud or my Legos. During those childhood moments, I was Ratovoantany. I was creating to create. I was creating for no particular reason other than perhaps to make the world more interesting by inflicting myself upon it.

That's the role of the artist. I don't mean emulating Ratovoantany, but rather, emulating a child. Ratovoantany is, for all intents and purposes, a child who, in his loneliness, is left to explore, to wonder and to grow from that wonder.

This is where it gets interesting because in every piece of artwork I create, there is what I call a magic moment. This is when a piece of art mysteriously goes from "okay" to "Holy Toledo! This is great!" Sometimes it's a stroke of paint, a change of color, an addition of an object. Whatever it is, it is something unexpected and exciting. If that experience doesn't happen, then the piece is not finished. It's where mud pies turn into something of worth—not financial worth, but soul-inspiring worth.

Zanahary is crucial to this process. Zanahary symbolizes that magic moment to Ratovoantany. The clay figures were cool, but with a breath of life, they became amazing. This is the meeting point of heaven and earth. It is the place where the base objects connect with something divine and otherworldly. This is Art, with a capital "A."

CLAY BEGINNINGS

Heaven and earth. I have to figure out how to portray *heaven* and *earth*. When I first envisioned this work, I imagined part of it being made out of clay. I envisioned a clay figure growing out an amorphous clay base. Nothing says earth like clay. One problem. I hate clay. It's not really my medium, plus it's unseeminly heavy. It's hard for me to guess how it would work with the other found objects. It might crack. I don't really know. Clay is out.

I do know that I will use one of those bajillion plastic anatomy men I have stashed away as the clay figure; I'll just add

some texture and paint to make it look like clay. What about the earth blob that I want the figure to rise from?

This is a job for Great Stuff foam insulation. It is great and extremely light . . . and airy, like a soufflé. Not to mention it's incredibly easy to model and paint to look like rock and earth.

Great Stuff is fun to use, but I have learned my lesson. Never again will I apply this goop without latex gloves. Time and time again, I got the stuff on me and I had to use pumice to scrape it off. Messy!

Time for the big foam. Little man is in place, and then, a sound vaguely reminiscent of shaving cream coming out of a can. Now I'll set it aside, because it's when you mess with it prematurely that you get in trouble. So time to walk away. In fact, I won't be back to this piece for at least a day. One of the hardest things for me to do is to jump from

DOLLAR STORE

ANATOMY MAN— When I was a kid, I remember periodically coming across those Invisible Man models. You know the ones: clear bodies so you could see all the internal organs. I did own a few of them, but I never made it to the assembly part. Truth be known, I was a horrible model builder. I had the best intentions, but when it came right down to it, I just didn't have the patience to assemble all the parts. I don't actually think I ever completed one. I take that back; there was a Dracula model I did finish, but not very tidily. The seams were all screwed up, and somewhere along the way I lost some of the pieces. Funny thing is that those old Aurora monster models were easy to assemble; not nearly as complex as model airplanes or "Star Wars" X-Wing fighters. I just don't like rules, I guess. Especially ones in instruction-manual form.

Back to invisible men. I was always amazed by these guys but knew that there was no way I could ever finish one. So decade piece to piece. Typically, I like to hunker down and work a piece straight through. Sometimes this is not possible. I am extremely impatient when I work on art. I'm a bit like Veruca Salt from *Willy Wonka and the Chocolate Factory*. I want it now. I want things to be ready when I want them to be ready. So I better take a chill pill and get something else done today.

I ordered some mannequin hands—about ten of them—and I'm a bit bummed because I thought they would be a bit larger. I assumed they would be life-size, which I guess they are, but child life-size. Not really what I was looking for, but for this piece, one will work, so I plop the hand on top. This will be Zanahary's hand of creation. It could also be the hand of Ratovoantany making the clay figures. Either way, it is the symbol representing the formation of the world and/or the elements of the world.

So a day goes by. The "stuff" is dry and it's time to get down to some serious art making. I take a craft knife and start slicing into the foam, and then tear portions of it. I want to get rid of the shaving cream look and turn it into rock. The floor around me looks like a movie theater after a scary movie. Yellow popcorn shapes are everywhere; a more anal person would stop and clean up the mess. Not me. I have work to do. I have paint to add in order to really "earthify" the piece. I start with a wash of Quinacridone Gold. (When don't I?) I add the same color to the little man. It is really important that it looks like he is part of the terra matter, and that the terra matter is part of him.

The top portion of the piece needs to be darker. It needs to be night. So black is the color of the moment; it won't stay that color, but it mentally lays out a plan of action.

Nice thing about those anatomy men is that they are complete with internal organs, though I very seldom use all of the guts. Something

after decade passed, and Michael lived his empty life, never knowing the joy of the Invisible Man, Woman or Cow. I had more or less forgotten about them, that is until my friend, Thomas Wynn (husband to the famous artist Jane Wynn), was teaching some classes using these guys. I noticed that the ones he was using were about half the size of the originals, and I asked him where he got the goods. He mentioned the Dollar Tree, and to boot, they were already assembled. Bear in mind, they are not particularly well made, but who cares; they were a buck.

I started making little assemblage anatomy men (à la déMeng, mixing various found objects into the mix) and next thing I know, people are going crazy. First off, they buy all my little creations, and then they start buying up all the dollar anatomy men. People were walking out of the Dollar Tree with shopping carts filled with these things. Crazy. Suddenly, the nude see-through dudes are becoming a rarity; time to take

119

This certifies that the fire equipment was

about spleens and intestines is really gruesome (which, by the way, was my complaint about the recent remake of the movie *Dawn of the Dead*—no intestine-eating zombies. If you are going to have a good zombie movie, they can't just gnaw on limbs, it's got to be internal organs for the full gross-out effect—but I ramble). Since I am not a zombie moviemaker, and I usually don't want to creep out my visual audience, I usually use only one organ, and that is the heart. Thanks to Mexican art and Frida Kahlo, the heart is somehow less creepy (even when it is portrayed in its accurate, non-valentine form).

I think the heart needs to feel separate from the clay-like body. I make it red; this will create a symbolic distinction between body and soul.

A little decorative painting, but it needs more junk. I have some metal bookplates (the things that you print books from) that someone dropped off to me. I find one with a design on it that would look pretty snappy behind the little dude.

On the shelf is this old piece of art. It was supposed to be for the cover of an album that some friends of mine were producing, but surprise, surprise, the band broke up and there it still sits on

my shelf. One of the parts is a rotary phone dial that I added an ear image to. I decided to take the big deconstructive step and rip the dial off. I'll like it better on this new piece (or so I hope). One never knows for sure . . . till it is too late.

Yep. A good move. It looks excellent placed on the little mannequin hand. Symbolically, it will be the ear of Zanahary, when he senses Ratovoantany making little clay figures.

I need to do something with the upper part. I have managed to get the lower part to the earthy tones I like, but the black, as I suspected, is too severe. Payne's Gray is a nice color when you add a bit of white; it produces a really nice indigo color. So I add a bit of this. In fact, I'll even bring a little of this color into the earth and body. Stellar. Speaking of stellar, some little dots above the man might be a nice touch to create the mood of stars and the heavens.

action. Every man for himself. So I start filling my own shopping carts with these guys. I think I purchased over a hundred of them.

Now they are all boxed up and holed away in my bomb shelter. One never knows when the dark cloud of nuclear war will make those things hard to come by. Then, after years of radiation exposure and mutations, the day will come when the tiny anatomy men will rule the earth. Kind of scary; I wonder if they are meat eaters. Maybe I'll keep them in a shelter separate from mine.

HOME IMPROVEMENT STORE

GREAT STUFF— I am renowned for using things in a manner that they are not designed for. In fact, I have been known to use the Dremel tool to cut a piece of string (my scissors were hidden under piles of junk, and the Dremel was handy). This is not really what I'm talking about, though. Sometimes you find a product that has some really interesting effects that can be

Time for the trademark, cutout eyes. What the piece really requires is something in which the color contrasts with the gray/blue color. I need a yellowish orange for this. I have found that old portraits from the 1700s offer a skin tone that has a fireplace glow. Nice and warm. In my studio is a book of such portraits that was purchased for a few bucks. It is almost intact, except for the multitude of little rectangles of eyes that are missing throughout.

A few more things here and there and actually, it's looking pretty good. It's almost done . . . maybe.

Three weeks later. I have not touched the piece in a while. It was supposed to be finished; however, with the passage of time, I have decided that this piece sucks. Not entirely, but it is really annoying me. Every time I look at it, I feel ill. I get this way. If a work of art is not perfect, it's a big pile of poop. Right now, that is exactly what it is. Poop with a capital "P."

It's passable, but I want more drama. It needs some zing to it. One thing I am aware of is that sometimes it is the most minute change or addition that can complete a piece. It could be as simple as a red dot. A good place to begin.

I take swatches of color and lay them on the piece, hoping that maybe a red (or a blue or a yellow) dot is all it needs. Nothing seems to do the trick. Now I know more extreme measures need to be taken. Let's try objects. I start grabbing various thingies. Gears. Wire. A wind-up, cymbal-playing monkey (I actually don't have one of those in my studio, but I would really like to someday). What about this? A weird, swivel-frame thing that I bought at the dollar store. Hey, pretty nifty! It will frame the bust of the man nicely. Plus, anytime you add a window it creates more intrigue; people want to look in. So there better be something in there to make the peek worthwhile.

applied to art. One such product is called *Great Stuff,* which is an insulating foam sealant. It is designed to fill in holes and gaps and seal them up. Well, sure, I suppose you could use it that way.

For me, the product is an excellent way to make rock-like formations. I could always attach real rock formations to the artwork, but why deal with the extra weight? *Great Stuff* is light as a feather.

It comes out like shaving cream, but it actually looks like yellow intestines. Now, since I don't often use yellow intestine imagery in my work, I have to do a bit of modification to the foamy stuff. A bit of whittling with a craft knife, a bit of tearing with my hands to rough it up... Then I add some paint and a few washes of color... Voilà, rock formations.

That frame magically eliminated all the composition issues. Amazing, if I do say so myself. Sometimes you think a piece is done, and other times you know it. I have finally reached the point where I know it.

I decree that the Zanahary piece is no longer poop. It is now a work of art. Now that is what I call alchemy. From poop to art. Not unlike the myth itself: from clay to existence.

The Handy-Dandy Resource Guide for the Secret Society of Trash-to-Treasure Hunters

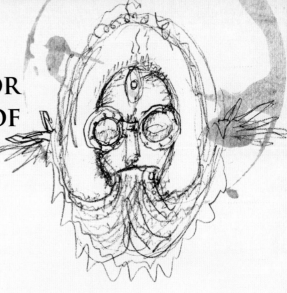

Liquid Planet

How does one start the day without a quadruple macchiato (espresso topped with a dollop of foamed milk)? Well, I don't know how the rest of you do it, but this is where my gusto comes from. I don't think I could have written a book without these friendly baristas.

223 N. Higgins, downtown Missoula, MT

www.liquidplanet.com

Ace Hardware

After all Ace *is* the place. This is where I buy most of my hardware goodies. Seems like at any given time there are hundreds of eager employees willing to offer assistance as well as problem solve. Half the time, however, it's a little hard to explain what you want to do with what it is you're looking for. When it come to art, there's a real-world/art-world disconnect.

www.acehardware.com

Home Resource

This place is a must for the Missoula junker. A great bunch of home recyclers. It's great when you can go into a place and say you need a bunch of thingies for art projects and their eyes light up. Check out their annual Spontaneous Construction art competition in the late summer.

825 West Kent Avenue, Missoula, MT

www.homeresource.org

Pacific Steel and Recycling

If you like getting your hands dirty and wandering through alleys of rusty metal and mud, then this is the place for you. You can't go here without thinking about Thunderdome.

2600 Latimor, Missoula, MT

Dollar Tree

Hey, everything's a dollar; how can you beat that? Think of it this way, for twenty bucks you can walk out with a basket of weird stuff. Who cares if it isn't quality-crafted? It will be dismantled and re-mantled into art!

www.dollartree.com

University of Montana Bookstore

If you can't get it there, they will find it for you. Not to mention that they are used to some of the most unusual art-project queries from students, so there are no worries of coming up against the blank expression that implies, "What do you want to do that for?"

University of Montana campus, Missoula, MT

www.umtbookstore.com

American Science and Surplus

From magnets to gas masks to map measurers, if you can't find something weird to buy . . . then you're weird. Great catalogue and online store, and a super great sense of humor.

www.sciplus.com

Circle Square Second Hand

This is a great store. The only problem is that all the other found-object artists in Missoula know it, too. You've got to be quick to get the goods.

519 N. Higgins Avenue, Missoula, MT

www.2ndhand.com

INDEX

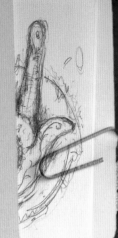

Eye of Fatima (name its different...
2. resin hand (find Jewish version...

INDEX CONT.

WHO IS THIS GUY?

First Memory: A gecko on a window
First Movie (remembered): *Billy the Kid vs. Dracula*
The Most Beautiful Thing Ever: An evening cemetery in Oaxaca during Dia de los Muertos

Michael deMeng Mumbo Jumbo

Gently add very encouraging parents.
Stir in a fascination for Dracula and the T.V. series *Dark Shadows*.
Agitate with a series of childhood relocations.
Let sit in the San Francisco Bay area till full-grown.
Add 1 part natural talent to 9 parts love for art.
Move ingredients to Missoula, Montana.
Add 5 years of art school.
Spread with acrylic paint.
Let simmer for a few years.
Add a dash of collage.
Stir in some Joseph Campbell.
Expose to Mexican art and traditions.
Mix in a healthy dose of Liquid Nails (original formula).
Add Shrines and found objects.
Place in blender.
Serve in various galleries and teaching venues around the world.
Garnish with a sense of humor
Voilà
deMeng Mumbo Jumbo

DeMeNG

INDULGE YOUR CREATIVE SIDE
WITH THESE INSPIRING TITLES FROM NORTH LIGHT BOOKS

These books and other fine North Light titles are available at your local craft retailer or bookstore or from online suppliers.

Artist Trading Card Workshop
Bernie Berlin

Find instruction and ideas for using a variety of mediums and techniques to make artist trading cards to collect and swap. Whatever your crafting background, you'll find innovative artistic techniques for making cards, including collage, painting, metal working, stamping and more. These gorgeous miniature works of art are a great way to introduce yourself to a new medium—and to make friends along the way. The book even offers suggestions for starting your own artistic community to trade techniques and cards.

ISBN-10: 1-58180-848-8
ISBN-13: 978-1-58180-848-3
paperback • 128 pages • Z0524

Pretty Little Things
Sally Jean Alexander

Learn how to use vintage ephemera, found objects, old photographs and scavenged text to make playful pretty little things, including charms, vials, miniature shrines, reliquary boxes and much more. Sally Jean's easy and accessible soldering techniques for capturing collages within glass make for whimsical projects, and her all-around magical style makes this charming book a crafter's fairytale.

ISBN-10: 1-58180-842-9
ISBN-13: 978-1-58180-842-1
paperback • 128 pages • Z0012

Metal Craft Discovery Workshop
Linda and Opie O'Brien

Discover a nontraditional approach to the introduction of working with metal and create 20 fun and funky projects. This is the whimsical side of metal that not only teaches you how to cut and join metal surfaces, but also allows you to explore ways to age and add texture to metal, conjure up beautiful patina finishes and uncover numerous types of metal such as copper, mesh, wire and recycled material. Whether you've worked with metal before or you're new to the medium, give your recyled tin cans a second glance and start crafting beautiful pieces with metal today.

ISBN-10: 1-58180-646-9
ISBN-13: 978-1-58180-646-5
paperback • 128 pages • 33235

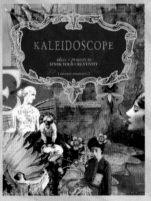

Kaleidoscope
Suzanne Simanaitis

Get up and make some art! *Kaleidoscope* delivers your creative muse directly to your workspace. Featuring interactive and energizing creativity prompts ranging from inspiring stories to personality tests, doodle exercises, paper dolls and cut-and-fold boxes, this is one-stop-shopping for getting your creative juices flowing. The book showcases eye candy artwork and projects with instruction from some of the hottest collage, mixed-media and altered artists on the zine scene today.

ISBN-10: 1-58180-879-8
ISBN-13: 978-1-58180-879-7
paperback • 144 pages • Z0346